JOY

John Fisher

BROADWAY PLAY PUBLISHING INC
New York
www.broadwayplaypublishing.com
info@broadwayplaypublishing.com

I0140300

JOY
© Copyright 2007 John Fisher

Cover art from the original Off-Broadway production
First printing: July 2007
I S B N: 0-88145-344-7
Book design: Marie Donovan
Word processing: Microsoft Word
Typographic controls: Ventura Publisher
Typeface: Palatino
Printed and bound in the U S A

JOY, originally titled THE JOY OF GAY SEX, was first presented at the University of California, Berkeley in November 1993. This production transferred in 1994 to Theater Rhinoceros, San Francisco. It subsequently transferred to the Bayfront Theater, San Francisco and the Actors' Theater, San Francisco for extended runs in 1994 and 1995. JOY in San Francisco was produced by Jon Zimmerman. JOY was produced in Los Angeles at the Saint Genesius Theater in 1999. All these productions were directed by the author. The cast and creative contributors for the San Francisco production were as follows:

CHRISTIAN . . . . Christian Milne
JANE . . . . Jane Paik
COREY . . . . Corey Schaeffer
MATT/ADAM . . . . Matt Schmidt
KEGAN . . . . Kegan Stedwell
DARRYL . . . . Darryl Stephens
PAUL . . . . Paul Tena
ELSA . . . . Elsa Wolthausen
CAL* . . . . Cal Grant

subsequently combined with the role of COREY

Director . . . . John Fisher
Choreography . . . . .Jane Paik
Musical direction . . . . James Dudek
Scenic & costume design . . . . June Chan
Lighting design . . . . Michael Habicht
Sound design . . . . Doug McCorkle

JOY opened in New York on 14 August 2005 at the Actors Playhouse, produced by Sean Mackey, Eva Price and Ben Rimalower. The cast and creative contributors were:

COREY . . . . Ken Barnett
DARRYL/MATT .Michael Busillo
CHRISTIAN . . . . Ben Curtis
KEGAN . . . . January LeVoy
ELSA . . . . Brooke Sunny Moriber
JANE . . . . Jane Paik
GABRIEL . . . . Christopher Sloan
PAUL . . . . .Paul Witthorn

Director . . . . .Ben Rimalower
Choreography . . . . .James DeForte
Musical direction . . . . Mark Hartman
Scenic design . . . . Wilson Chin
Costume design . . . . David Kaley
Lighting design . . . . .Ben Stanton
Sound design . . . . Zach Williamson

The set: JOY is performed on a simple set which consists of an open stage with a large picture frame up-center, and, if possible, a flight of stairs which lead off the front of the stage on which actors can sit and talk intimately with the audience where required. In the picture frame appear panels which depict the central image of each scene: the Golden Gate Bridge, U C Berkeley's campanile, the pedestrian pier, a panel of red velvet for the opera, etc. These panels shift a vista and are part of the action. They should be cartoony images, fun. The furniture consists of two short benches and a table which are shifted as needed. There are a number of "low tech" effects: the panels, the moon over the pier, the BART train, etc. The spotlight is also crucial. These are part of the show and a reminder that this is a play being presented with a limited budget, even if the budget is large. Call them "camp" effects.

The music: Aside from the original music of this production, several commercial recordings are indicated. These can be replaced by other music or variations on the show's songs, as desired, so long as the mood of the songs indicated is replicated.

Casting: JOY is performed by five men and three women. One actor plays both MATT and ADAM. In the original production an American southern accent was used for MATT.

The Performance: JOY should be performed with an air of irony. The characters know they're being dramatic. They are having fun living this story. They talk to the audience because they enjoy the drama of their lives and want to communicate it. As a matter of fact, PAUL's problem is that the likes to have fun, often at other's expense, and it gets him in trouble. Without this sense of irony, or dislocation, the play can be too earnest, too sincere, which it is not meant to be.

ACT ONE

1:1

(A view of the Golden Gate Bridge which, as you know, is actually red. GABE, in a spotlight, sings the refrain of "Misery" which we will hear later in its entirety. He wears a white dinner jacket and black tie. PAUL, in another spot, watches him. PAUL is dressed more casually. When GABE finishes the refrain his spot fades, but the music continues. PAUL addresses the audience.)

PAUL: Joy. Or, as it was originally titled, The Joy of Gay Sex. Tonight's presentation is perhaps inappropriately named for it will not serve as a how-to manual for the uninitiated. The Gay Sex of the title is lamentably not a reference to the glorious acts of sodomy, fellatio, felching, rimming, and others, too numerous to mention. The Gay Sex is a reference to the third sex; not male, not female; gender designations which are defined by their opposition to their procreative partners. The Gay Sex is not concerned with procreation, not pressured by it. It is the sex defined only by desire. For how can there be anything but desire when the need to reproduce, the need to further the species, is removed from the realm of interpersonal relationships. Such needs will take care of themselves. They are a function of instinct. But desire, pure desire unencumbered by need, is that which lifts man above the animals. It creates culture. And it is for this reason that the Gay Sex is the most human, the most sophisticated, the least animal of the sexes. Male and female are for the earth. The Gay Sex can lift us up, up to the stars.

(PAUL *gestures to the heavens and, indeed, we see stars alight. Perhaps a shooting star cuts through the cosmos.*)

PAUL: This story takes place on a star. A little star on a bay. This star is connected to the animal kingdom by a couple of highways and two bridges—one of them is red. (*He gestures to the bridge.*)

(*We hear The Pet Shop Boys' remix of* Go West *quietly playing in the background. As* PAUL *speaks the rest of the cast file on-stage in the dimly lit area behind him.*)

PAUL: By the end of the millennium this star had suffered many setbacks, but it was reasserting itself and it showed signs of becoming, once again, the brightest star in the firmament. To this star I came. I was, of course, a member of the Gay Sex, but I had known no joy. This is the story of how I found joy on that not so distant star.

(*The disco music blares as loud as possible. The stage explodes with light—lasers, flashing lights, mirror ball etc. Revealed in the flashing lights is a stage full of sweating dancers gyrating wildly to the music. At the center of this activity is* PAUL, *still in his spot, and gyrating more wildly than the rest. The dancing continues for a full minute. Then* PAUL *steps down-stage of the dancers as the dancers continue their dance up-stage. Whenever* PAUL *speaks the music becomes quieter.*)

PAUL: (*To the audience*) San Francisco. 1994. I was gay. I was single. I was dancing in the Castro. (*He returns to the dancing momentarily.*) I loved San Francisco. Sodom and Gomorrah? Maybe. But I didn't believe in Sodom and Gomorrah. At least not the one that God destroyed because it was full of fags. As a matter of fact I was writing my dissertation about that. About Biblical

attitudes, old testament and new, towards
homosexuality. But the best part was the final
chapter in which I argued, persuasively, that Christ
himself was a fag.

(PAUL *gyrates some more and then the music fades, the disco
lights fade and the dancers begin to fade away.*)

PAUL: The number ended and I went home. Alone.
I wasn't horny that night. Just tired of reading,
analyzing, synthesizing. So I treated myself to a
night out. Not to be ruined by thoughts of finishing
my degree or getting laid. I wasn't lonely. Just alone.
Which, I'd decided, must be how I'd been meant
to spend my life. If I craved anything it wasn't sex,
but companionship. Now I'm maudlin. (*Cheering up*)
But I wasn't that night. I'd been dancing and now I
was going to pick up a movie. So I stopped by Tower
and picked up a movie.

1:2

(PAUL *catches a Tower bag which is thrown to him from off
stage left. He holds it up.*)

PAUL: (*To the audience*) Dumbo. Nice story. Nice songs.
Short. A little bit racist. But, overall, a good movie.
I headed home. (*He moves towards stage right.*) But as
I passed Café Flore I heard—

(*In an instant the lights bump up center stage to reveal
COREY and GABE sitting at a small table. In front of them
is coffee.*)

COREY: Paul!

PAUL: Corey!

COREY: Come. Sit!

PAUL: (*To the audience again*) Corey. A professor from school. We were in the same program together—Ancient History. And, yes, we'd slept together—also Ancient History. He was writing about Agrarian Reform in Tuscany in the Late Roman Empire. Not the faggiest of subjects. I was always telling him that I felt it was the duty of every faggot historian to write about faggot issues in history. He felt it was the duty of every faggot historian to keep a low profile, get grants and secure a job at a major university. We argued. We stopped sleeping together. But we were still friends.

COREY: (*Spreading his arms gaily*) Darling!

(COREY *and* PAUL *kiss flamboyantly.*)

PAUL: (*To the audience*) Of course, in the Castro, he could be a queen.

COREY: This is Gabriel.

PAUL: (*To the audience*) Not exactly chicken, I thought, but cute.

GABE: (*With a nice smile*) Hi.

PAUL: (*To the audience*) And a very sweet smile.

COREY: Sit, sit, sit.

(PAUL *and* COREY *sit down with* GABE. *Of course, whenever* PAUL *speaks to the audience everyone else on stage freezes.*)

COREY: What are you up to?

PAUL: I've just been out dancing and now I'm headed home with *Dumbo*. You two on a date?

(COREY *and* GABE *suddenly look uncomfortable.*)

COREY: (*Changing the subject*) Ah, no... We've just been to see *Death in Venice*. At the Castro.

PAUL: *(Disgusted)* Oh no, not that Visconti mess.
The one with Dirk Bogard?

COREY: Yes.

PAUL: Oh, please. That thing is the lamest piece of
gay film-making. Completely devoid of eroticism.
And that kid playing Tadzio, the one with the rock-
and-roll haido. Oh honestly—did you believe for a
moment that anyone was infatuated with that kid.
He looked like he never washed his hair.

GABE: I liked it.

PAUL: *(To* GABE*)* Do you see many movies?

(Silence. GABE *looks offended.)*

PAUL: Look, I'm kidding. What did you like about it?

GABE: I thought it was very touching.

PAUL: Have you seen *The Damned*?

GABE: No.

PAUL: Now that's Visconti's fag movie. Nazi's in drag.
Lots of cute boys running around. Horrible family
situations. Lots of self-loathing sex. *Death in Venice*
is crap.

(Another silence)

GABE: I liked it.

PAUL: *(To the audience)* So I wasn't making the very best
first impression. He wasn't that cute anyway. So fuck
him.

COREY: *(Changing the subject)* Tomorrow they're
showing *Jesus of Montreal.* Have you seen that?

PAUL: Yeah. How about you?

COREY: No, not yet.

PAUL: Don't bother. It's all about how every woman in Montreal falls in love with this young actor playing Jesus. In other words, it's another movie about straight actors. Isn't that fascinating? How innovative! It's complete dreck.

GABE: I liked it.

PAUL: *(Giving* GABE *a withering stare)* Do you believe in straight actors?

GABE: What?

PAUL: Do you believe in straight actors?

GABE: I don't understand the question.

PAUL: Do you believe they exist?

GABE: Oh come on.

PAUL: How about this. Do you believe in a straight Jesus?

COREY: Can we please not get started on that.

PAUL: *(To* COREY*)* Excuse me. I'm interested. *(To* GABE*)* Do you believe that Jesus was straight?

GABE: Again, I don't understand the question.

COREY: Paul's has this theory that—

PAUL: It's not a "theory". You make it sound like something I thought up on the way over here. *(To* GABE, *a speech he's made before and often)* I'm writing my dissertation on old and new testament attitudes towards homosexuality and one of my premises is that Christ himself might have very well been gay or at least predominantly homosexual as we would define it today and—

GABE: Wasn't he celibate?

PAUL: What? Are you kidding?

GABE: I always thought he was celibate.

PAUL: Do you really believe in celibacy?

GABE: But he's Christ.

PAUL: Oh come on. Do you honestly believe that someone can be celibate his whole life?

GABE: Well he couldn't possibly be gay.

PAUL: Why not?

GABE: Because he was a Jew and the Jewish bible forbids homosexuality.

PAUL: *(Slams the table)* Yes, of course. The Old Testament. The Old Testament forbids homosexuality. Everyone's a biblical scholar. You're going to start quoting Leviticus to me and the story of Sodom and Gomorrah. Listen, Leviticus is not a condemnation of sex with boys but of sex with temple prostitutes. It all comes down to the mistranslation of a single word. *"Toevah"*.

COREY: Which any Hebrew scholar would read as a very simple and clear-cut condemnation of homosexuality.

PAUL: Yes, but I'm not a Hebrew scholar. I'm a gay scholar.

COREY: It's a Hebrew text.

PAUL: And I don't read Hebrew?

COREY: That's not my point.

PAUL: Do I read Hebrew?

COREY: Look, I'm tired of talking about this.

PAUL: *(Pounding the table to emphasize each word)* Do I read Hebrew?

COREY: Yes, yes, you read Hebrew.

PAUL: Thank you. *(To* GABE*)* It's a mistranslation.

COREY: Then how come Hebrew scholars have never caught it.

PAUL: They have their agenda and I have mine. *(To* GABE*)* I'm not the only one who thinks this. *(To* COREY*)* How do you explain King David fagging around with Jonathan? Just really good friends? Like Cary Grant and Randolph Scott?

COREY: They were teenagers. David ended up married with children.

PAUL: Only because Jonathan died. David was devastated. How do you explain Christ's love for John? John told everybody that Christ loved him.

COREY: You're confusing love with penetration.

PAUL: Do you believe in love *without* penetration? *(To* GABE*)* Do you?

GABE: I'm very confused.

PAUL: There's nothing to be confused about. *(To the audience)* And then I made a big mistake. *(To* COREY *and* GABE*)* You know what I don't understand? I don't understand why a couple of fags like you two wouldn't want to believe that Christ himself was gay. *(Silence)* I mean, why is that? *(Silence. To the audience)* Something was definitely wrong. But, with infinite grace, I bullied on. *(To* GABE*, obnoxiously)* You are gay aren't you?

GABE: *(Unconvincingly)* No.

PAUL: *(To the audience)* Oh, come on. *(To* GABE*)* Oh come on. *(Silence)* You're joking right? *(Silence. To* COREY*)* He's joking right?

COREY: I don't know. *(To* GABE*)* Are you gay?

GABE: No.

(PAUL *bursts into laughter at* GABE'*s pronouncement.* GABE *turns away in annoyance and crosses his legs at the knee. This petulant gesture only makes* PAUL *laugh all the harder.* COREY *and* GABE *look uptight. Eventually* PAUL *calms down and looks embarrassed. They all stare at their coffee.*)

COREY: (*Trying to salvage the situation*) Did you see *Lawrence of Arabia*?

PAUL: Now that... That's a good movie. Nice story. Good acting. Lots of gay subtext. (*To the audience*) And then, arriving in the nick of time, was Kegan.

(KEGAN *enters from stage right alone and looks for a table.*)

PAUL: (*Calling to her*) Kegan!

KEGAN: Paul!

PAUL: (*To the audience*) Kegan was also in my program. She was a feminist.

KEGAN: (*To the audience*) Ah, no, I am not a feminist. I write about women in history. "Feminist" is a marginalizing term. Like "faggot". (*To* PAUL) Are you a faggot?

PAUL: Yes.

KEGAN: Well, that's the difference between us. You embrace your marginality. I do not. Hi Corey.

(*She kisses* COREY *on the head.*)

COREY: Hey Kegan.

PAUL: (*To* KEGAN) You here alone?

KEGAN: No, I'm here with Christian.

PAUL: Where is he?

KEGAN: (*Looking around*) Missing.

(CHRISTIAN *enters from right.*)

KEGAN: There he is. Christian!

(CHRISTIAN *crosses towards them.*)

KEGAN: Get lost?

CHRISTIAN: *(Clearly lying)* Ah, yeah.

KEGAN: *(To* PAUL*)* This always happens when we come to the Castro. *(Indicating for* CHRISTIAN*'s benefit)* This is Paul and Corey and someone I don't know.

GABE: Gabriel.

CHRISTIAN: Hi.

COREY: *(Putting on his sunglasses)* Hi.

PAUL: *(To the audience)* It was immediately clear that Corey was in love with him.

COREY: *(To* PAUL*, indicating the audience)* Why did you tell them that?

PAUL: Because you just put on your sunglasses.

COREY: What the hell difference does that make?

PAUL: It's odd. It's the middle of the night. You might as well have told him to his face.

COREY: He has no idea.

PAUL: Believe me, he knows.

COREY: He has no idea.

PAUL: *(To the audience)* He knew.

COREY: *(To the audience)* He had no idea.

CHRISTIAN: *(To the audience)* I had no idea.

(COREY *smiles at* PAUL *then turns back to* CHRISTIAN.)

COREY: Hey, man. You a student?

CHRISTIAN: Yeah.

COREY: You should check out my seminar: Ancient Ethics.

(COREY *sits down and spreads his legs suggestively open towards* CHRISTIAN.)

CHRISTIAN: *(To* COREY*)* I will. *(To* KEGAN*)* I have to go to the bathroom.

KEGAN: Great. *(Pause)* Don't be too long.

(CHRISTIAN *exits stage left.* KEGAN *sits down at the table.*)

PAUL: *(To* KEGAN*)* Will he be alright?

KEGAN: Oh yes. He's been going to the bathroom for years.

PAUL: Are you dating?

KEGAN: Yes. He's very flexible. Did you hear, *Jesus of Montreal* is playing tomorrow night. Cool movie.

GABE: *(Standing up)* You know, I should get going. I have classes tomorrow.

COREY: *(Also standing)* Yeah, so, we're leaving.

KEGAN: *(To* COREY*)* Are you two on a date?

PAUL: Gabriel's straight.

KEGAN: Oh come on.

(PAUL *and* KEGAN *burst out laughing.* GABE, *frustrated, strikes another poncey pose.* PAUL *laughs even more. Eventually he controls himself.*)

GABE: *(Angrily)* It was a pleasure meeting both of you.

PAUL: *(Trying to control himself)* Yes, I mean, I'm sorry.

KEGAN: I guess I'm sorry too. *(To* COREY*)* He knows you're gay, doesn't he?

COREY: Well, he does now.

(PAUL *and* KEGAN *burst into hysterics again.* COREY *gets up.*)

COREY: *(To* GABE*)* You all set?

GABE: I think so.

COREY: *(To* KEGAN *and* PAUL*)* Bye.

(As COREY *and* GABE *are exiting stage left.)*

COREY: Where are we parked?

GABE: I don't remember.

(And they are gone.)

KEGAN: That was completely weird.

PAUL: Makes perfect sense to me. Corey's half closeted so he dates fully closeted men. They're trying to avoid marginalization.

KEGAN: Gabriel's going to be marginalized whether he likes it or not. He might as well enjoy some sex.

(They continue to laugh. CHRISTIAN *appears beside* KEGAN*.)*

CHRISTIAN: I'm back.

KEGAN: Good work. *(To* PAUL*)* Isn't he cute?

PAUL: Mmmm.....

KEGAN: He's one of my students. And he's also very bright. *(To* CHRISTIAN*)* Tell Paul what you had to say about *Candide.*

CHRISTIAN: I liked the part where he stuck the bayonet in his butt.

(Pause)

KEGAN: *(To* PAUL*)* You see what I mean?

PAUL: Mmmm...

KEGAN: *(Standing)* So, we're off. Call me.

PAUL: But of course. *(To* CHRISTIAN*)* I'll see you.

CHRISTIAN: Bye Gabriel.

PAUL: I'm Paul.

KEGAN: *(To* CHRISTIAN*)* Gabriel was the gay one. *(She winks at* PAUL*.)*

CHRISTIAN: Bye Paul.

PAUL: Bye Christian.

KEGAN: *(To* CHRISTIAN *as they exit)* How was the bathroom?

CHRISTIAN: Ahh... *(And they are off.)*

1:3

PAUL: *(To the audience)* And so I met Gabriel. I have to say I wasn't terribly impressed. Twenty, twenty-one year old closet case with lame opinions about film and Christianity. And he didn't seem to be aware he was on a date with Corey. I really did feel bad about laughing at his professed sexual orientation. *(He begins laughing again and, in time, stops.)* Anyway, between Kegan and Corey and the nubile Christian, I really didn't think that much about Gabriel. I assumed I'd never see him again and left it at that. A week later—the scene shifts to a campus on the other side of the bay. *(The panel shifts to reveal a picture of U C Berkeley's campanile.)* The eastern side. Although it was technically a part of the animal kingdom, this campus was more of an oasis in that kingdom, a satellite, a lesser star in the orbit of San Francisco's sun. It was here that I toiled as a graduate student and it was here that I saw Gabriel once again.

*(*GABE *crosses from up left to up right singing ABBA's* Dancing Queen *to himself.* PAUL *watches him.)*

PAUL: I thought nothing more of it than "Oh, his name is Gabriel." A week later he passed on the sidewalk. He was in a hurry.

(GABE *passes him quickly crossing from down right to down left.*)

PAUL: I thought, "Oh, there goes what's-his-name." Meanwhile, Kegan, who was not a feminist but was a budding lesbian, met someone at a crosswalk.

(ELSA *enters from stage right, crosses to center and stands facing the audience.*)

PAUL: She was very sweet and she was waiting to cross the street. I give you "Kegan Meets Elsa— A Pantomime." Corey.

(PAUL *signals to* COREY *at the piano.* COREY *plays some sinister music which suggests an animal stalking its prey.* KEGAN *enters from stage left and crosses to stand beside* ELSA *down center.* KEGAN *glances at her, notices her beauty and decides to stare at her.* ELSA *realizes she is being stared at and acts embarrassed. Slowly she begins to enjoy being stared at and she tries to stare back without seeming obvious.* KEGAN *just stares.*)

PAUL: (*To the audience*) This went on for about fifteen minutes. It was one of those self-serve crosswalks— no light to hold the traffic for the pedestrians. They just stood there waiting for a break in the traffic. Elsa finally just crossed the street. She chickened out first. (*To* ELSA) Thank you.

(ELSA *exits stage right.*)

PAUL: Kegan, I'd found, was one of the few people I could talk to in my program. She usually slept with undergraduate boys, but then she started telling me about the ubiquitous blond with the perfect skin. (*He has now moved in next to* KEGAN.)

(ELSA *crosses from stage right to stage left without noticing or hearing* PAUL *or* KEGAN.)

KEGAN: (*Pointing at* ELSA) Look, that's her.

PAUL: Who?

KEGAN: The one I was telling you about. She's incredible.

PAUL: *(To the audience)* This seemed to happen every time Kegan and I got together.

(ELSA immediately crosses in front of them going the other way. She stops down center. She is obviously waiting for someone.)

KEGAN: *(To PAUL)* There she is.

PAUL: *(To KEGAN)* Ah yes. Miss Right.

KEGAN: She's incredible. Look at her.

(ELSA is very natural.)

KEGAN: She's so natural. She's got style.

PAUL: Nice hair.

KEGAN: The hair's amazing.

(ELSA shifts her weight from her left leg to her right leg.)

KEGAN: Oh my God, I love the way she shifts her weight. Wait, look at this. She does this all the time. This thing with her hair.

(ELSA runs her hands through her hair.)

KEGAN: Un-fucking-believable.

PAUL: She looks like she's so nice.

KEGAN: I know. Do you think I'm too tough for her?

PAUL: You? Oh no.

(Suddenly CHRISTIAN appears beside them.)

CHRISTIAN: Kegan. Hi.

KEGAN: *(Startled)* Hi.

CHRISTIAN: *(Rubbing her arm)* How are you?

KEGAN: I'm fine. Get lost.

(CHRISTIAN *looks hurt and exits.*)

KEGAN: The whole world makes sense when I look at her. Everything falls into place. The planet spins slower. The air smells fresher. Every animate and inanimate object is suffused with passion, purpose and poise. She is style. She is woman. I look at her and I leave behind the cobwebby remains of my middle-class sexuality and embrace a sexuality of life, being, humility and desire. She is the beginning, middle and end of all existence and I but a poor suppliant wretched, degenerate and tawdry. I adore her though I do not know her name.

(GABE *enters and kisses* ELSA *on the cheek.*)

PAUL: My God, that's what's-his-name.

KEGAN: Who?

PAUL: The little fag from Café Flore. The one Corey was trying to nail.

KEGAN: Her boyfriend.

PAUL: He couldn't be. That'd be too funny.

(ELSA *and* GABE *exit stage right.*)

KEGAN: They're leaving. What do we do?

PAUL: Follow them.

1:4

(KEGAN *and* PAUL *head off right.* KEGAN *exits right, but* PAUL *turns back to the audience.*)

PAUL: And so we followed them to the Engineering Library where, it seems, they both worked re-shelving books.

(PAUL *exits quickly stage right. We hear the sinister stalking music again—this time a greatly sped up version.*)

(ELSA *enters from stage rights miming as if she were pushing a library book cart.* KEGAN *and* PAUL *enter as if they were following her. She works her way stage left up and down many "aisles of books."* KEGAN *and* PAUL *follow her movements always staying one "aisle" behind her.* ELSA, *having arrived at her desired aisle stage left, performs a series of shelving actions.* KEGAN *and* PAUL, *observing these actions from between the books of an "aisle" just stage right of* ELSA's, *comment on* ELSA's *actions.*)

KEGAN: She's incredible.

(ELSA *stretches up to place a book on a top shelf.* KEGAN *enjoys the view this move affords of* ELSA's *butt.*)

KEGAN: Oh my God, that looks great.

(ELSA *stretches even higher with a small kick and then comes to rest on the flat of her feet.*)

KEGAN: Oh, God, that was intense. I almost had an accident.

PAUL: She's a great dresser.

KEGAN: Never wears the same outfit twice. She's coming back this way.

(*They run back into another "aisle" as* ELSA *moves her cart into the "aisle" that they formerly occupied.*)

PAUL: This is ridiculous.

KEGAN: Shut up. If she sees me I'll scare her off.

(GABE *enters from stage right pushing a mime book cart and maneuvers it into an "aisle" stage right such that he and* ELSA *are sandwiching* PAUL *and* KEGAN.)

PAUL: Damn. Here comes the other one.

KEGAN: I think she's moving into our aisle.

PAUL: Well we can't back up one.

KEGAN: Why not?

PAUL: I don't want to run into that kid.

KEGAN: Why not?

PAUL: Because I made a total ass of myself the first time I met him and I can't remember his fucking name and I don't want to run into him right now thank-you-very-much.

KEGAN: Would you keep your damn voice down.

GABE: Elsa?

ELSA: Yes, Gabriel.

KEGAN: *(To* PAUL, *enraptured)* Her name's Elsa.

PAUL: *(Mocking* KEGAN*)* His is Gabriel.

GABE: Are we supposed to have three copies of Kostoff in the stacks?

ELSA: No. One of them goes on two hour reserve.

GABE: Oh.

PAUL: What if he comes into our aisle?

KEGAN: Well, we can't go into her aisle.

PAUL: What the hell are we supposed to do then?

KEGAN: Well you can back up one but I'm not going to.

PAUL: *(Taking* KEGAN's *hand)* Come on. *(He pulls her around into* GABE's *aisle. To* GABE, *in a whisper)* Hi.

GABE: *(Aloud)* Hi.

PAUL: Shhh... We met in the city a few weeks ago. You were with my friend Corey. My name's Paul.

GABE: *(Whispering)* Yes, I remember. Why are we whispering?

PAUL: Well Kegan is totally in love with Elsa and we're sort of following her. You know.

GABE: *(Excited)* Oh, that's great, I love things like that.

KEGAN: She's incredible.

GABE: Yes, she's very special.

PAUL: Anyway, we thought you might be able to help us out.

KEGAN: You're not her boyfriend or anything?

GABE: Oh no.

ELSA: Gabriel.

(GABE, KEGAN and PAUL are stunned into silence.)

ELSA: Gabe? *(Silence)* Are you all right?

PAUL: Answer her.

GABE: What do I say?

KEGAN: Just cover.

GABE: *(In a cracking voice)* Yes?

ELSA: Are you all right?

GABE: Yes, Elsa, I'm fine. Don't come over here.

ELSA: *(Amused)* I wasn't planning on it.

GABE: Good, good.

ELSA: What are you hiding?

GABE: Nothing, nothing.

ELSA: I heard whispering. Who are you hiding over there?

(She moves towards GABE, PAUL and KEGAN.)

GABE: No, don't come over.

KEGAN: Damn!

(KEGAN *ducks around the corner into another "aisle"*
leaving PAUL *behind with* GABE.)

GABE: Elsa, don't come—

(*And* ELSA *has arrived at the end of the aisle and is staring*
at PAUL *and* GABE. PAUL, *in the panic to escape, has*
inadvertently placed his hands on GABE's *waist. This is the*
position ELSA *catches them in.* PAUL *quickly pulls his hands*
away.)

ELSA: Oh, hi. You are with someone. Am I intruding?

GABE: No, no, this is Paul.

PAUL: Hi. (*Pause*) I'm Paul.

GABE: We're friends.

PAUL: From the Castro.

(GABE *gives* PAUL *a dirty look.* PAUL *realizes what he has*
said and looks embarrassed.)

GABE: (*Trying to change the subject*) Paul's an historian.
Ancient History right?

PAUL: (*Nervously babbling*) That's right. Well, actually,
ancient Judea. Well, actually I'm writing about King
David and Jesus—that crowd.

GABE: And Sodom.

PAUL: And Sodom.

ELSA: (*Amused*) Got it. Well, just so long as you boys are
all right.

GABE: Oh, we're fine. How are you?

ELSA: I'm fine. Well, see ya.

GABE: Yes, thank you.

PAUL: Pleased to meet you.

(*And* ELSA *returns to her cart.*)

GABE: *(To* PAUL*)* Well, she doesn't think she's being followed.

PAUL: No.

KEGAN: *(Rejoining them from her hiding place)* She has the most adorable voice. And she says the most adorable things. "See ya." Adorable.

GABE: Can we move this discussion to my desk? This is getting a little too nerve wracking.

PAUL: *(To the audience)* So we moved the discussion to his desk.

(PAUL, KEGAN *and* GABE *take a single large step to down center. This brings them to* GABE's *"desk".)*

KEGAN: *(To* GABE*)* Is she gay?

GABE: I don't think so.

KEGAN: Is she seeing anyone?

GABE: Not at present. No.

KEGAN: Good. So here's the situation. I ran into her a couple of weeks ago on a street corner and I tried just staring at her but nothing came of it. She was obviously enjoying herself but then she diffused the situation and ran off. So she has some impulses but she also has some hang-ups, right?

GABE: I'd say that's a fair assessment.

KEGAN: So my sense is she's not going to respond well to any aggressive behavior. Nothing like an overt come-on, right?

GABE: No, she wouldn't go for that.

KEGAN: So how should I approach her?

PAUL: You have to contrive some recurring situation wherein you two are forced to spend a lot of time together.

KEGAN: Like a class or something.

PAUL: Yes.

GABE: She takes a dance class every day.

(*This amuses* PAUL. KEGAN *gives him a dirty look.*)

KEGAN: What time?

GABE: Six o'clock.

PAUL: So, you'll take the dance class?

KEGAN: I guess I'll have to. (*To* GABE) Thank you so much. You've been a complete doll.

GABE: Oh please. I love intrigue.

(KEGAN *and* PAUL *move left as* GABE *moves right.*)

KEGAN: (*To the audience*) So that semester I learned how to dance. But before leaving Paul that day I said (*To* PAUL) That kid's great.

PAUL: Yes, very helpful.

KEGAN: And cute.

PAUL: You think so?

KEGAN: I do. Great smile.

(*And she walks off.* PAUL *stands thinking.* ELSA *crosses to* GABE.)

ELSA: (*To* GABE) I liked your friend.

GABE: Paul? Oh, I barely know him.

ELSA: You two seem very comfortable together.

GABE: You're trying to embarrass me.

ELSA: No I'm not. I'm just teasing.

GABE: You're going to tell me for the four hundredth time this month that I'm gay.

ELSA: No. You're the one who keeps saying you think you might be gay. I just agree with you.

GABE: Do you think I'm gay?

ELSA: Straight men do not whisper in the aisles with cute boys.

GABE: You think he's cute?

ELSA: I do.

PAUL: *(To the audience)* And thus transpired the interlude in the library. *(To* GABE *and* ELSA*)* Thank you.

*(*GABE *and* ELSA *exit stage right. The lights dim to a spot on* PAUL.*)*

1:5

PAUL: *(To the audience)* It is now time to address my nemesis.

(We hear some ominous and terrifying music—very Darth Vader. Red lights slowly rise on COREY.*)*

PAUL: Doctor Corey Cabinoff. Boy wonder. At thirty he was already a full professor at the University of California. Recipient of the National Book Award for History. Two Pulitzer Prizes for Non-Fiction. An Academy Award for Best Adapted Screenplay. A Fulbright. A Ford. Two Guggenheims. A MacArthur. And the Nobel Prize for Literature. And, yes, the third reader on my dissertation committee.

COREY: *(To* PAUL*)* Paul!

PAUL: *(To* COREY*)* Corey!

COREY: Doctor Cabinoff on campus, Paul.

PAUL: Doctor Cab. Sounds like a drink. How was New York?

COREY: Fine, thank you.

PAUL: Congratulations on your profile in *Vanity Fair*. Is it true about you and Susan Sarandon?

COREY: We're friends.

PAUL: The article made it sound like you two have coitus.

COREY: We have the same publicist. While I was in New York I had Denise fax me a copy of your final dissertation proposal. *(He reads from a fax memo.)* "Our Accepting Father: Overtones of Homosexual Love and Permissiveness in the Old and New Testaments With an Aside to the Predominant Sexual Tendencies of Jesus Christ." *(To* PAUL*)* Now what made you think I would let you get away with that?

PAUL: That's right, you wrote the book on Jesus Christ didn't you?

COREY: I wrote a book on Jesus Christ. A very influential one. And there's no way you're going to convince me that he was a homosexual.

PAUL: Oh, come on. He was a Roman citizen. Everyone in the Roman Empire was fagging around with everyone else all the time.

COREY: *(Growing angry)* The evidence for homosexuality in ancient Rome is scanty. The evidence for it in ancient Judea is non-existent.

PAUL: And any attempt to find it in the Bible is blasphemous?

COREY: *(Angry)* It is a problematic assertion, yes.

PAUL: No more problematic, it seems to me, than your Nobel Prize winning assertion that Christ, through most of his life, was high as a kite on marijuana.

COREY: *(Furious)* My assertions were based on fiber samples from the Shroud of Turin.

PAUL: And if anybody ever produces Christ's underpants I'll prove conclusively that he was a faggot!

COREY: *(Seething)* All right Paul, just remember, you brought this on yourself.

PAUL: Brought what on?

COREY: Well, if you're going to write about Jesus Christ, you're going to have to read the Sanskrit texts.

PAUL: In the English translations?

COREY: *(Wickedly)* No! In the original Sanskrit!

PAUL: *(To the audience)* Learn Sanskrit, the salt-mines.

COREY: *(Savagely)* Sanskrity!

PAUL: *(To the audience)* It was this closet case's way of punishing me for writing about a faggot Christ.

(CHRISTIAN appears to the right of COREY.)

CHRISTIAN: Doctor Cabinoff!

COREY: *(Beaming at CHRISTIAN)* Christian! My new student.

CHRISTIAN: *(Brown nosing it)* Congratulations on your *Vanity Fair* profile. You look great in a Speedo

(COREY and CHRISTIAN laugh like queens.)

COREY: How's your paper on Agrarian Reform coming Christian?

CHRISTIAN: Splendidly.

COREY: We should have dinner some time. Next Tuesday?

CHRISTIAN: Fine.

COREY: I know this little place on Market Street. We can discuss your...bibliography.

(They giggle.)

CHRISTIAN: Oooooo... You're wicked.

COREY: *(To PAUL)* Paul, *dum spiro spero.* Go in peace. *(He touches CHRISTIAN.)*

CHRISTIAN: Ethics, Professor. Ethics. Wait till we're off campus.

(They both giggle wildly and then assume straight postures and exit. The lights dim to the spot on PAUL.)

1:6

PAUL: *(To the audience)* Kegan wasn't much of a dancer. But she always worked up a sweat and put on a good show for Elsa.

(The lights come up stage left to reveal ELSA and KEGAN executing their dance exercises. They both sit on the floor and face the audience as if they were looking in a dance studio mirror. KEGAN sits on the floor just up stage of ELSA so that she can look at ELSA. We can also hear GABE and DARRYL singing a section of "Misery" as COREY accompanies them on the piano. PAUL stands in his spot and watches ELSA and KEGAN. At first ELSA is very diligently executing her moves and KEGAN is intently watching her. Then ELSA executes a turning move and notices that KEGAN is staring at her. KEGAN quickly pretends to be doing her exercises.)

PAUL: Anyway, that night Kegan and I were off to see "Tosca" at the opera. So I waited outside the dance hall.

(The lights dim to black on KEGAN and ELSA.)

PAUL: And as I waited I heard two ethereal voices floating down the hall from another rehearsal room. One of the voices was oddly familiar.

(The lights fade up on GABE *and* DARRYL *singing at the piano with* COREY *accompanying them.)*

PAUL: I crept down the hall and opened the door to the rehearsal room and there I beheld the specter of Gabriel. He was a singer.

*(*GABE *and* DARRYL *complete the song.* PAUL *applauds their performance.)*

GABE: *(To* PAUL*)* Oh, hi.

PAUL: *(To* GABE*)* Hi, that was wonderful.

GABE: *(Embarrassed)* You think so?

PAUL: Oh yes, you've got a beautiful voice.

DARRYL: *(Butting in)* Thank you.

GABE: But it's such a dumb song.

PAUL: Oh no. I'm a real sucker for soppy music. Especially the way you sing it.

GABE: Thank you.

(For the first time they really look at each other. Silence)

COREY: *(Deliberately breaking the spell)* Paul! So good to see you again.

PAUL: Oh, hi Corey.

COREY: Hard to believe there are other people in the room.

PAUL: And who knew you fondled the ivory.

COREY: I'm a Renaissance man, Paul.

PAUL: Bitalented?

COREY: This is Darryl.

PAUL: Hi Darryl.

COREY: He's straight Paul.

PAUL: *(Through clenched teeth)* Thanks Corey.
(To DARRYL*)* You have a lovely voice also.

DARRYL: Thanks.

GABE: We normally sing these songs with Elsa.

PAUL: She's a singer also?

GABE: Yes. She got us an audition for the Black-and-White Ball and we're trying to get as many songs under our belt as possible.

PAUL: The Black-and-White Ball. *(Not impressed)* Wow.

GABE: I know, it's kind of tacky. But it's a good gig. And we'd get into the ball free.

PAUL: Well, if you're singing, I'll come.

GABE: It's a hundred dollars to get in.

PAUL: *(With bravado)* I'll swing it. I don't know many celebrities.

GABE: *(To* DARRYL*)* So now we're celebrities.

DARRYL: The big time.

*(*DARRYL, GABE *and* PAUL *laugh.)*

COREY: *(Annoyed)* Can we maybe go through this again? I have to be somewhere.

GABE: Oh. yeah, sure. *(To* PAUL*)* I have to get back to work.

PAUL: Yes, I'll get lost. *(He has a thought.)* Listen, do you like Opera?

GABE: Opera? Yeah, sure.

PAUL: 'Cause Kegan and I are going to see *Tosca* tonight and, you know, maybe you'd like to come.

GABE: *Tosca?*

PAUL: *Tosca.*

GABE: Well. I'm meeting Elsa after dance class.

PAUL: That's perfect then. Bring her along. Kegan would love it.

GABE: I guess she would.

(COREY *and* DARRYL, *who know what's going on, strike up a romantic song as subtle background music to* PAUL *and* GABE's *conversation.* GABE *gives them a look. He looks back at* PAUL. PAUL *is smiling broadly.*)

GABE: *(Embarrassed)* Isn't it expensive?

PAUL: We stand.

GABE: Oh, well that sounds cool. *(Eagerly to* COREY*)* We're done here right?

1:7

(COREY, *without looking up from the music, nods his head.* PAUL *and* GABE *exit stage right.* COREY *continues his accompaniment and the lights go down on stage right as they come up on* KEGAN *standing stage left.* ELSA *enters from left and crosses towards right until* KEGAN's *shout stops her.*)

KEGAN: *(Incredibly loud)* Hey!

(*She crosses to* ELSA *whom she has frightened. The music cuts out with the "Hey!")*

KEGAN: Listen, I don't understand half the shit we're doing in there and I thought maybe you could help me out with it sometime.

ELSA: *(A little reluctant)* I'd be happy to.

KEGAN: How about right now?

ELSA: I don't think I can. I'm supposed to meet my friend Gabriel. We're going to go out.

KEGAN: Oh. What are you going to go do?

ELSA: I don't really know.

(KEGAN *waits for an invitation.*)

KEGAN: OK, well, maybe some other time.

ELSA: Yeah, sure, remind me.

(PAUL *and* GABE *enter from right laughing.*)

PAUL: *(Crossing grandly to* KEGAN*)* Kegan, we're off to the opera. Gabriel's going to join us. Isn't that marvelous?

GABE: *(To* ELSA*)* Yes, Paul invited me and I said we'd be happy to join them.

ELSA: Wait. You all know each other?

PAUL: Yes, we go way back. But introductions will be made in the car. La Tosca awaits.

(PAUL, GABE, KEGAN *and* ELSA, *standing in this order from stage right to stage left, walk down stage into the "Opera Lights."* COREY *plays the romantic music as they cross. The panel changes to one of an opera poster for a production of* Tosca. *They stand as if they were standing in the standing room area at the back of the orchestra section at the San Francisco Opera.*)

PAUL: The seats directly in front of us cost one hundred dollars each. Ours cost eight.

KEGAN: They're sitting down.

PAUL: We're Bohemian, they're bourgeois.

GABE: The price of middle-class complacency is high.

PAUL: Well said, dear Gabriel.

(GABE *and* PAUL *smile.*)

ELSA: *(Looking around)* Can you believe all the face-lifts in this place?

GABE: They're intense.

KEGAN: Oh, I'm all for face work. The second I have
any money—bang—I'm having everything done.
Nose, chin, tits, buttocks.

ELSA: But you have such a nice face.

KEGAN: Thank you.

PAUL: I just want to have my hairline frozen.

GABE: I'd just like to have my forehead smoothed.

ELSA: Well I think plastic surgery is totally shallow.

KEGAN: That's because you are completely adorable
and could not possibly be improved upon.

ELSA: Yeah, right. You're just flattering me.

KEGAN: No I'm not. I've been following you for weeks.
Haven't I boys?

PAUL: That's right.

GABE: 'Fraid so.

PAUL: *(To the audience)* Elsa didn't blush. She just smiled
ever so imperceptibly and turned towards the stage.
And Kegan, noting this, smiled ever so broadly and
faced the stage. There now followed the most sublime
performance of *Tosca* I had ever seen.

(The lights dim a little bit and we hear the finale of Tosca.
The actors now stare out as if they were watching the opera.)

PAUL: I can't remember the soprano's name. She wasn't
famous. Nor was the tenor. But their love story was
absolutely convincing. And when Tosca threw herself
off the Castel Saint Angelo, Gabriel grabbed me.

(And GABE *gasps and grabs* PAUL.)

PAUL: And my brains turned to whipped-cream.
The power of art.

(The music becomes thunderous as if the orchestra was playing in the theatre itself. It reaches a tremendous climax and then PAUL, GABE, KEGAN *and* ELSA *begin applauding and clapping wildly. They have clearly enjoyed themselves.)*

KEGAN: *(Overwhelmed)* That was devastating.

GABE: *(Forlorn)* I want to go to Rome.

ELSA: *(Through tears)* I hate opera. That was great.

KEGAN: God, what are we going to do to follow that?

GABE: *(To the audience)* And then Paul had this great idea.

(We hear the strains of After the Show.*)*

PAUL: I drove to the top of Telegraph Hill.

ELSA: And we walked down the Filbert Steps.

KEGAN: In the moonlight.

GABE: Out across Levi Plaza.

PAUL: Along the piers.

GABE: And out onto the Pedestrian Pier where we looked at the lights of the Bay Bridge reflected in the Bay.

(The panel changes to one of the San Francisco Bay Bridge lit up at night and reflected in the water of the bay.)

PAUL: And the Transamerica Pyramid soaring up behind us.

ELSA: And Coit Tower soaring up above it.

KEGAN: Isn't it beautiful?

GABE: Yeah, it's really—really so pretty late at night with all the lights on.

PAUL: Oh, I know. I love it.

ELSA: Boy—

KEGAN: Hmm.

PAUL: This is really a great city. I don't care what anybody says. It's just so—really a knockout, you know?

GABE: But everybody thinks it's a knockout.

PAUL: That's true.

KEGAN: *(To the audience)* And then Elsa started to sing.

(ELSA sings the first line of the refrain of After the Show. *GABE joins her for the second line and then KEGAN and PAUL join in for the third and fourth. On the fourth line the two couples join hands and begin to walk up-stage hand in hand. They arrive up stage and turn to point at a small moon which has risen above the set or from one of the wings. They stand in tableau and enjoy the romantic moon as the lights fade to black. Soon the lights fade up to reveal ELSA and GABE standing in front of the Campanile picture.)*

1:8

ELSA: What are you thinking about?

GABE: Just what a great time I had last night.

ELSA: I was thinking the same thing.

GABE: What else were you thinking?

(ELSA only smiles.)

GABE: What?

ELSA: That—

GABE: That?

ELSA: That she's so...tough.

GABE: And?

ELSA: And I like it.

GABE: *(Nudging her)* You.

ELSA: What about Paul?

GABE: What about Paul? I mean, I really don't know what to do.

ELSA: You should get a hold of him.

GABE: He'll get a hold of me. I left my backpack in his car.

ELSA: That's so cute.

PAUL: *(Entering from right)* Hello there.

GABE: Oh, hi Paul.

PAUL: I came to return your backpack.

GABE: So where is it?

PAUL: Ooops. I must have left it at home. Damn. Well, you'll just have to come by and collect it then. At eight P M. Sharp. That's 520 Sycamore. Don't be late. *(To* ELSA*)* Have fun in dance class, Elsa.

1:9

(And he exits right. The lights dim to leave ELSA *in a spot light center. She crosses to left.* KEGAN *walks into* ELSA's *spot.)*

ELSA: *(Getting* KEGAN's *attention)* Hey! *(*KEGAN *turns to her.)* You mentioned you were having problems with some of the things we've been doing in class. We could do some now.

KEGAN: *(Taking* ELSA *by the arm)* Fuck that, let's get a drink.

(The spot swings to stage right. PAUL *enters the spot spraying his apartment with air-freshener. We hear the doorbell ring.* PAUL *gives a quick spray under his arms,*

hides the air-freshener and then GABE *steps into the spot from right. He is holding a bottle of Martinelli's.)*

GABE: Well, here I am.

PAUL: Well, here you are.

(The spot shifts to left where KEGAN *and* ELSA *are sitting on a bench. They both hold cocktails.)*

ELSA: I had a crush on all my baby-sitters. And all my best friends. And then, when I was eleven, my friend Ellen and I had sex. We kept having it until I was fifteen. Then we stopped.

KEGAN: What happened?

ELSA: Ellen found out it was sex.

KEGAN: What happened to her?

ELSA: She didn't speak to me for three years. Now she's at Mills.

KEGAN: I'm shocked. I would never have guessed you had this history.

ELSA: Oh, I do everything to suppress it. It was very traumatic.

KEGAN: Was it?

ELSA: Yes, I'm extremely closeted.

KEGAN: *(Disappointed)* Oh.

ELSA: *(Reassuring her)* Politically. Not sexually.

KEGAN: Oh good.

ELSA: I wonder how Paul and Gabriel are doing.

(The spot shifts to right where PAUL *and* GABE *are sitting on the other bench kissing intensely.)*

GABE: *(Breaking)* Look, I'm just not sure I'm ready for this.

PAUL: *(Grabbing him)* Neither am I.

(PAUL resumes kissing him.)

GABE: *(Breaking)* I mean, I'm not sure that I'm gay.

PAUL: *(Grabbing him)* Good, I hate fags.

(PAUL resumes kissing him.)

GABE: *(Breaking)* But—

PAUL: What?

GABE: *(After a thought)* Nothing. *(He resumes kissing PAUL intensely.)*

(The spot shifts to KEGAN and ELSA left.)

ELSA: *(Rubbing KEGAN's thigh)* Sex ruins things.

KEGAN: I know.

ELSA: Would you like to come over?

KEGAN: *(Excited)* Yeah.

(The spot shifts to right where PAUL and GABE are now under a sheet as if they are in bed. They are sharing a cigarette. They look at each other and sigh contentedly. Then they laugh. The spot shifts to left where KEGAN and ELSA are under a sheet as if they are in bed.)

ELSA: First time?

KEGAN: Yeah. Is that bad?

ELSA: No.

KEGAN: How could you tell?

ELSA: A couple of times you seemed at a loss.

KEGAN: I didn't know what to do with my legs. I hope you don't get a black eye.

ELSA: It didn't hurt. Really.

KEGAN: I was so embarrassed.

ELSA: It's like riding. You have to get into the habit.

KEGAN: Has there been anyone since Ellen?

ELSA: No. But once you've done it, you never lose the knack.

(The spot shifts to GABE *and* PAUL *under their sheet kissing.* GABE *looks up from the kiss and looks annoyed. He waves the spot away. It shifts back to* KEGAN *and* ELSA *under their sheet.)*

KEGAN: Listen, do I have to keep coming to dance? I hate it.

ELSA: I don't like it either. I just go there to meet women.

KEGAN: Cool.

(The spot shifts to GABE *and* PAUL *who are now under their sheet so that we can only see the sheet and hear their voices.)*

GABE: Mmmm. What's this position called?

PAUL: It's called State Penitentiary.

GABE: Ohhhhhh.....

(The spot shifts to KEGAN *and* ELSA *who have also disappeared beneath their sheet.)*

KEGAN: Mmmm. That feels great.

ELSA: Yeah, the gravy ladle was a good idea.

(The spot shifts to center to reveal COREY *and* CHRISTIAN *under a third sheet.)*

COREY: Christian, that was wonderful?

CHRISTIAN: Thanks, Professor.

COREY: Corey.

CHRISTIAN: Corey. Sorry.

COREY: Was this your first time?

CHRISTIAN: No such luck. I was a regular slut in high school.

COREY: You seem so virginal.

CHRISTIAN: It's an act.

COREY: It's a real turn-on that act.

CHRISTIAN: Yeah, I like your instructor routine. Very convincing.

COREY: Roll over. I'll show you something I teach in Latin.

(The spot shifts to PAUL *and* GABE *whose heads are now visible above their sheet once again.)*

GABE: You can stay if you want to.

PAUL: This is my apartment.

GABE: Oh. Can I stay?

PAUL: But of course.

(The spot shifts to DARRYL *who is under his own sheet and talking on the phone.)*

DARRYL: Mom, I'm on the other line... Yeah, sure... *(He clicks the hold button. In a sexy voice)* Now what did you say you were wearing?

(The spot shifts to KEGAN *and* ELSA *with their heads visible above their sheet again.)*

KEGAN: I'm just going to stay here all right? Because this is the happiest I've felt in about ten years and I don't want to go home and deal with my miserable single existence just yet.

ELSA: Yeah, sure, fine.

(The spot shifts to PAUL *and* GABE.)*

GABE: *(Teasing)* I thought you were a total creep the first time I met you.

PAUL: I know. It's one of my charms.

GABE: Did you pursue me?

PAUL: Not exactly. I feel like I succumbed to fate.

GABE: Mmm. That's nice.

(The spot shifts back to KEGAN *and* ELSA.*)*

KEGAN: I'm falling asleep.

ELSA: Good.

KEGAN: *(Waking up suddenly)* So I have to tell you that you're incredibly special and that my life has been completely useless up to this moment and that if I don't see you tomorrow night I know that I will sink back into the swill of mediocrity and malaise that I have called my life up to this moment and that that will probably necessitate an act of self-destruction on my part.

ELSA: Fine, we'll go out tomorrow night.

KEGAN: And there will be more sex right? I mean, I wasn't so virginal and amateurish that you didn't enjoy it and you'd like to keep the relationship on a dinner and movie basis from now on.

ELSA: It was amazing. Look, I have to get up in forty-five minutes. Go to sleep now.

(The spot shifts to COREY *and* CHRISTIAN.*)*

COREY: *(Confessional)* Christian, I think I'm falling in love with you.

CHRISTIAN: *(Disgusted)* What?

COREY: Ah, nothing.

(The spot shifts to KEGAN *and* ELSA.*)*

KEGAN: *(Panicked)* Elsa!

ELSA: *(Drowsy and annoyed)* What?

KEGAN: I insist that this is not the end of my sexual life as a lesbian. If I am inadequate I want to know now. If I am adequate I want some sort of guarantee that I will be given future opportunities to improve in the hopes that one day I will prove worthy of your experience.

ELSA: Would you please shut-up.

KEGAN: I'm talking too much.

ELSA: Yes.

KEGAN: *(to the audience)* She hates me.

(ELSA *kisses her gently on the cheek. The spot shifts to* PAUL *and* GABE.)

PAUL: *(To the audience)* I will lock the door and never let him go. He is here for life.

(PAUL *and* GABE *kiss tenderly. They both turn to face the spot and give a gentle blow in its direction. The spot, as if it was a candle, is blown out. Almost immediately the lights come back up on* PAUL *and* GABE *who are now sitting on the steps down center.* GABE *is sitting a step down from* PAUL *in* PAUL's *arms.)*

1:10

PAUL: *(To the audience)* And three weeks later my lovely Gabriel moved in.

GABE: *(To the audience)* He wouldn't take no for an answer.

PAUL: Which is funny because before Gabriel I'd always been afraid of living with someone. I was afraid they would ruin my rhythms, prevent me from getting anything done, and just shift everything around in an annoying way.

GABE: Which is exactly what I did.

PAUL: And I loved it.

GABE: He lived in a complete pigsty. Filth everywhere and he only ate pizza and Lucky Charms.

PAUL: He taught me how to cook. He made me take a shower everyday. We got stoned every night. I stopped work on my dissertation all together and we did nothing but talk, watch movies and have lots of sex.

GABE: The sex was great. The movies terrible. After that little treatise on Visconti and *Jesus of Montreal*, you'd think he had refined tastes in movies. No. He watched the worst crap imaginable.

PAUL: *(Proudly)* I like historical drama from Hollywood's Golden Age.

GABE: Which means four hour Charleton Heston movies I'd never heard of. *The Cid. The War Lord. The Egyptian.*

PAUL: Charleton Heston was not in *The Egyptian.* That was Victor Mature.

GABE: And war movies. Oh my God, war movies. *The Longest Day.*

PAUL: A great flick.

GABE: *Where Eagles Dare.*

PAUL: Even better.

GABE: And one day he made me watch this ninety-five hour catastrophe starring John Wayne and Patricia Neal—it was the most boring thing ever created—

PAUL: *(Gasps)* Don't you dare say mean things about *In Harm's Way.*

GABE: *In Harm's Way. (Screams with terror.)* Ahhhhh.....

PAUL: *(Playfully hitting him)* Stop it.

GABE: This thing had every tired incredibly ancient washed up movie actor in it. It was like watching Hollywood Squares: Burgess Meredith, Carol O'Connor, Dana Andrews. It was *The Towering Inferno* of war movies. And it was so boring.

PAUL: *(More hitting)* Stop it. Stop it. *(To the audience) In Harm's Way* is one of the three great creations of western civilization: the Venus de Milo, Beethoven's Sixth, and *In Harm's Way*. It is John Wayne's Lear.

GABE: Oh please.

PAUL: *(Excited)* It's all about John Wayne, who is this admiral during the Second World War, and Kirk Douglas is this total sleaze ball friend of his—

GABE: And the climax is this big naval battle between the Japanese and the Americans which looks like it was filmed in a Jacuzzi.

PAUL: That battle is one of the most moving pieces of choreography captured on film.

GABE: Paul, nobody is interested. That film is a catastrophe. Enough.

PAUL: John Wayne is a genius. The heavens parted, a light shown down, and there was John Wayne.

GABE: No. The heavens parted, a light shown down, and there was Fred Astaire.

PAUL: And Ginger.

GABE: Yeah.

(They both begin singing Cheek to Cheek *but they don't get very far because neither of them know the lyrics very well. They laugh and hug.)*

GABE: But mostly we just hung out and talked.

PAUL: *(Ironically)* And agreed on everything.

GABE: And we only left the house to work and shop.

PAUL: And he became my Gabey.

GABE: And he became my P P.

PAUL: *(Playfully)* Don't you dare tell them what that stands for.

GABE: And for the first time in my life everything made sense.

1:11

(The lights on GABE *and* PAUL *fade as a spot picks up* KEGAN *and* ELSA *dancing on from left. They are both wearing nice black dresses and are dancing to Bobby Darin's* Beyond the Sea. *About a third of the way through the recording the music fades and they continue to dance simple steps as they talk to the audience.)*

KEGAN: And we went on dating.

ELSA: Which was very nice.

KEGAN: *(To* ELSA*)* Paul and Gabriel have been living together for a month now.

ELSA: *(To* KEGAN*)* It will never last.

KEGAN: Two months.

ELSA: It's different for gay men.

KEGAN: Three months.

ELSA: They never go out. I can't live that way.

KEGAN: Four months.

ELSA: They never answer the phone. It must be stifling.

KEGAN: Five months.

ELSA: Fine. They're dead. Nobody's smelled the bodies yet.

KEGAN: Six months.

ELSA: I'm not ready.

KEGAN: They're happy.

ELSA: They're children. They've sealed themselves off from the real world. Of course they're happy.

KEGAN: *(To the audience)* And then there came the night when Paul and Gabriel threw a house warming party.

ELSA: *(To the audience)* They wanted to show off their domesticity.

KEGAN: *(To* ELSA*)* I don't think that was it at all. *(To the audience)* Elsa had refused to move in with me so was very sensitive on the subject of domestic bliss.

ELSA: *(To* KEGAN*)* I hadn't refused. *(To the audience)* I was waffling. Kegan had turned what was very casual and very nice into something very serious, very political. She wanted to advertise it to the world. I wasn't ready for that.

KEGAN: *(To* ELSA*)* So I'll wait.

1:12

(They execute one last complicated move as the music swells. The stage lights come up on PAUL *and* GABE*'s apartment which consists of the two benches facing one another.* PAUL *enters from right sipping a martini. He is wearing a very nice party dress and a large wig.)*

PAUL: *(To* KEGAN *and* ELSA*)* It was supposed to be a drag party. Why the hell aren't you two in drag?

KEGAN: *(To* PAUL*)* We are in drag. We wore dresses.

ELSA: I haven't worn a dress since the Ford Administration.

PAUL: *(Disappointed)* Oh, Christ. *(To the audience)* Finally that's what went wrong that night. Nobody in this burg seemed to know what a drag party is.

GABE: *(Entering in a dress and wig)* Kegan, Elsa, you wore dresses. That's hysterical. *(He strikes a pose.)* How do I look?

ELSA: Gabriel, you look beautiful.

KEGAN: You are fully marginalized.

PAUL: *(Embracing GABE)* Isn't he the cutest thing?

KEGAN: Adorable.

PAUL: And he cooks and cleans.

ELSA: *(To KEGAN)* Domestic bliss.

(PAUL moves to kiss GABE on the cheek and GABE screams and pulls away.)

GABE: Careful. Everything smears.

PAUL: He's taken to drag like a duck to water.

GABE: *(To KEGAN and ELSA)* Quack, quack.

(The doorbell rings.)

GABE: *(Falsetto)* Coming! *(And he runs off left.)*

KEGAN: *(To PAUL)* He seems very happy.

PAUL: He's happy. I'm happy.

GABE: *(Off)* Bon soir. *(Entering)* They've come.

PAUL: *(To KEGAN and ELSA)* Corey and Christian.

GABE: *(To off-stage left)* Well, come on.

(COREY and CHRISTIAN enter dressed, not too convincingly, as Mary Magdalene and Christ.)

GABE: Aren't they cute?

PAUL: *(After a beat)* I don't get it.

COREY: We dressed especially for you. I'm Mary Magdalene and Christian is Christ.

PAUL: *(After another beat)* Christian is not in drag.

COREY: Of course he is. Christ wore a dress. Sort of.

PAUL: Christ did not wear a dress. If Christian is dressed as Christ he is not wearing a dress. You've missed the point completely.

GABE: Oh Paul.

COREY: *(Fuming)* Look, I barely got him into this outfit so it will have to do.

PAUL: And I don't know what the hell you're wearing.

COREY: I'm dressed as a New Testament prostitute.

PAUL: That's pathetic. You couldn't possibly look less provocative.

KEGAN: I think they look spectacular. *(To* COREY *and* CHRISTIAN*)* I think you look spectacular.

CHRISTIAN: Thank you.

PAUL: Gabriel and I, by my reckoning, are the only people here in drag. I could not possibly be more disappointed.

GABE: Oh Paul.

PAUL: Would you please stop "Oh Paul"ing me. I mean look at them. I meant this party to be a liberating experience for my faggot friends. You all got dressed like you did it at gun point.

COREY: *(Near tears)* This is the only dress I could find in my size.

PAUL: Unacceptable. You should have told me. I know plenty of large drag queens who would have been only too happy to help you out. You've all failed me.

COREY: Incredible.

KEGAN: Could we maybe get something to drink?

GABE: I'll get it.

PAUL: No. I'll get it. I am the hostess. *(And he sweeps out grandly.)*

ELSA: Is he serious?

GABE: 'Fraid so.

KEGAN: *(Shouting after* PAUL*)* Asshole!

CHRISTIAN: Is something wrong?

KEGAN: Oh sweetie, everything's fine. You look great.

COREY: *(Even closer to tears)* I spent all day getting ready for this.

ELSA: So did we.

(The doorbell rings.)

GABE: Everything will be fine. Excuse me. *(He exits left.)*

COREY: I really can't believe this.

KEGAN: Well, it won't be the first party he's both thrown and ruined.

(GABE enters form left with DARRYL, who is not in drag.)

GABE: And here's Darryl.

DARRYL: Hi.

ELSA: *(Registering* DARRYL*'s attire)* Uh, oh.

GABE: I forgot to tell him.

DARRYL: Tell me what?

CHRISTIAN: Hi, I'm Christian. Where's your dress?

DARRYL: My dress? What are you guys talking about?

KEGAN: You'll find out soon enough.

DARRYL: You guys look great.

PAUL: *(Entering with a tray of martinis)* Martinis, martinis!

DARRYL: *(Responding to PAUL's outfit)* Woah, Paul.

PAUL: *(Seeing that DARRYL is not in a dress)* I don't believe it.

GABE: Now Paul don't get started. I forgot to tell him it was a drag party.

PAUL: *(Throwing up his hands)* That's it. That's it. We're going to put a stop to this right now.

(He hands the drinks tray off to ELSA.)

DARRYL: What's wrong?

PAUL: This has gotten completely out of hand. Gabriel, I want you to take Darryl into the bedroom and put him into a dress. If he resists, you are to do it by force. I'll send Christian in to help.

DARRYL: But—

PAUL: I'm not angry with you dear. I'm just angry. Gabriel, Christian, to work!

(GABE and CHRISTIAN begin dragging DARRYL off stage right.)

GABE: Come on, Darryl.

CHRISTIAN: It's best not to resist.

DARRYL: *(Struggling)* But I can't wear dresses. Really. My mother made me swear I'd never put on a dress.

(And the three of them exit right.)

COREY: You are unbelievable.

PAUL: I'm taking charge of a deteriorating situation. If history teaches us anything it's that at some point the minority must seize the initiative.

COREY: I don't believe in drag. I think it paints a degrading picture of homosexuality.

PAUL: Perhaps. I see it as a breaking down of gender roles as they are traditionally defined by clothing.

(He takes a martini from the tray, which ELSA *now holds. To* ELSA*)*

PAUL: Thank you. *(To* COREY*)* At any rate, even if it is degrading, one must do it with conviction or one becomes just plain lame. You know what? When they're through with Darryl we're going to send you in there for a complete make-over.

COREY: I'm taking this wig off. It itches.

PAUL: *(Seething)* Don't you dare.

(The doorbell rings.)

PAUL: Excuse me. *(He exits stage left.)*

ELSA: *(Realizing the disaster that is approaching)* Oh my God, that must be Matt.

COREY: Matt?

ELSA: A friend of mine from high school. He's in town for the weekend.

COREY: He better be in a dress.

KEGAN: *(Getting drunk)* Well, at least Paul knows how to mix a martini.

(We hear PAUL *scream with delight off. He comes onstage pulling* MATT *by the hand.* MATT *is in a full dress naval uniform.* PAUL *deposits* MATT *center stage and admires him.)*

PAUL: Oh Elsa, he's marvelous. Simply marvelous. And so tall.

*(*MATT *begins to remove his cap.)*

PAUL: Oh, no, you keep your hat on. I just love a man in uniform.

COREY: But he's not wearing a dress.

PAUL: Ah, but I figured it out immediately. He must be a real drag queen so this must represent some sort of drag transformation for him, *n'est-ce pas?*

ELSA: Ah, actually—

KEGAN: *(Jumping in)* Yes, Elsa, that must be it. *(Introducing everyone)* Now I'm Kegan. I'm Elsa's... friend.

MATT: Pleased to meet you ma'am.

KEGAN: And this is Corey and Paul.

MATT: *(Nodding to each in turn)* Sir. Sir.

PAUL: *(Giggling with excitement)* Oh, sit, sit. Elsa, he's priceless. Wherever did you find him? He's wonderful.

ELSA: We were in high school together.

PAUL: He's not a student is he? He's far too witty to be a student.

ELSA: Actually, he is. He's at the Naval Academy at Annapolis. Thus the uniform.

PAUL: *(After a beat)* What ?

ELSA: I tried to explain to him over the phone what a drag party was but I don't think he fully understood.

PAUL: *(Angrier than ever)* This is outrageous.

COREY: *(Loving this)* Ha, ha, ha.

GABE: *(Off right)* Well, here we come.

(GABE, DARRYL and CHRISTIAN enter from right. DARRYL is in a very short dress and wig. He seems to get a kick out of it.)

GABE: How did we do?

DARRYL: I think the skirt's a little short.

PAUL: *(Bette Davis at a party)* It is, you look cheap.

(GABE gasps and DARRYL looks crestfallen.)

PAUL: Gabriel, this is Matt. He attends the United States Naval Academy at Annapolis, which apparently entitles him to show up to my party inappropriately dressed.

KEGAN: Relax Paul.

PAUL: I will not relax. I spent my youth being bullied by macho shit-heads like this and I will not have him marching around here like it was the deck of the *U S S Kitty Hawk.*

ELSA: We better take off. Come on Matt—

PAUL: You will not take off, young lady. He wouldn't dare appear on the parade ground in a dress and he sure as hell is not going to get away with not wearing one here. Gabriel, I want you to take Matt into the bedroom and show him how we dress in San Francisco on a Saturday night.

ELSA: We're leaving. Come on Matt.

PAUL: *(Feigning tears)* Elsa, you have made a shambles of my party. Your presence here with this non-com thick neck in full dress uniform is an insult to the entire homosexual community.

ELSA: I brought him because I thought he'd have fun. I thought he'd get a kick out of a drag party.

PAUL: Oh yes. Come laugh at the faggots. What a sensitive notion Elsa. I live to amuse the straight community.

ELSA: That's not what I meant. I thought it'd be nice for him to meet some different people. He doesn't know anybody gay.

PAUL: I find that hard to believe. Annapolis is one of the faggier institutions in this country, the navy being the faggiest. I'm sure they're giving him a thorough training at the academy for all those long months at sea.

KEGAN: Now I want to leave.

PAUL: Oh, please, please do. All faggot haters and closet cases, now is your time to leave.

COREY: Anybody ever tell you you're incredibly paranoid.

PAUL: Daily. That doesn't mean people aren't out to get me.

(As the scene proceeds, CHRISTIAN *assumes the position of the crucified Jesus against the upstage frame.)*

DARRYL: This is ridiculous. *(To* MATT*)* Matt, just come into the bedroom, we'll put you into a little dress and everything will be fine. They've got a huge selection.

KEGAN: *(Stepping in)* No. I won't let you give in to these Gestapo tactics. *(To* MATT*)* I forbid you to put on a dress.

PAUL: If he doesn't put on a dress on I'll scream the house down.

COREY: That's it! We're leaving! *(To* PAUL*)* You're right, drag is not degrading. But standing here listening to this is. You conceive of the gay community as some kind of hermetically sealed vault which can only exist with the rest of the world on its terms. More precisely, your terms. Well you are not the spokesman for my gay community.

PAUL: *(Grandly)* A pretty speech. Exit stage left to thunderous applause.

COREY: *(To* MATT*)* I'm sorry this had to happen to you. My brother's in the Coast Guard.

PAUL: And the Coast Guard's in him.

COREY: *(Outraged)* Come on Christian, we're leaving.

CHRISTIAN: *(To* PAUL*)* Well, I don't really know you well enough to say anything nasty so *(And he gives* PAUL *a Bronx cheer and exits left.)*

PAUL: "Forgive them, Lord. They know not what they do."

KEGAN: *(To* ELSA*)* Let's go.

ELSA: We probably should.

PAUL: Yes, that's right. Show your solidarity with all "right thinking" homosexuals.

KEGAN: No, just with people who have class.

*(*PAUL *sings a line of* The Party's Over *drunkenly.)*

ELSA: *(To* GABE*)* Thanks for having us.

GABE: But Elsa—

ELSA: *(To* DARRYL*)* Are you coming?

DARRYL: No, I should probably change.

PAUL: *(To* ELSA*)* And waiting for him to change would ruin your exit.

ELSA: *(Exasperated)* Matt, put the tray down. We're leaving.

*(*MATT *hands the tray to* KEGAN *then turns to* PAUL*.)*

MATT: *(Politely)* Sir.

PAUL: Ma'am. *(As* MATT *exits left* PAUL *sings to his back and marches about drunkenly.)* "Anchors away my friend..."

KEGAN: That's it. I'm out of here. *(She heads out left holding the tray.)*

PAUL: Please leave the tray.

(The tray flies on from off left and lands center.)

PAUL: Thank you.

GABE: *(After a pause)* Well, that was a disaster.

PAUL: And rightfully so. It was shaping up into a miserable evening with nobody getting into the spirit of the occasion.

GABE: And now there's no occasion.

PAUL: No.

GABE: *(To* DARRYL*)* You better change.

*(*GABE *and* DARRYL *exit right. We hear Aretha Franklin's recording of* Drinking Again *as the stage lights quickly dim and a spot light zeros in on* PAUL. PAUL, *now alone in the spotlight, stares ruefully at his martini glass.)*

1:13

PAUL: *(To the audience)* So I like to have fun at parties. It took Gabriel three days to get over it. It took me four to realize I had done anything wrong. He didn't punish me in any way. He just seemed depressed and quiet. As Kegan pointed out, it wasn't the first party I'd unsuccessfully hosted. Every once in a while I blew some perceived insult out of proportion and systematically destroyed a potentially nice evening. And I always realized afterwards that I did it because I took some perverse pleasure in having that kind of control over a situation. It was fun. And people always forgive you in the end. Especially if you're extra contrite the next time around. But Gabriel threw parties because he liked to see people have a good time. And he could never understand why anybody would deliberately prevent that from happening. Ultimately, he just couldn't understand people being hostile to one another. It

didn't upset him, it only depressed him. And at the
end of the fourth day I began to wonder if maybe our
relationship was in jeopardy. He and Elsa had landed
that gig at the Black and White Ball. He was too much
of a gentleman to not invite me. But I could tell he
wasn't sure he wanted me there. I, of course, went.

1:14

(The spot shifts off of PAUL *to* GABE *who enters from left.
He is dressed in white tie and tails. The picture shifts to a
picture of San Francisco City Hall.* GABE *sings* Misery *in
its entirety. He is accompanied on the piano by* COREY *who
is also in white tie and tails. Half way through the song*
ELSA, *in very nice formal wear, joins him in the song.
Near the end of the number* PAUL *enters in white tie and
tails. The number ends and he approaches* GABE.*)*

PAUL: *(To* GABE*)* Hi.

GABE: How are you?

PAUL: That was beautiful.

GABE: It's a beautiful song.

COREY: *(From the piano)* Excuse me, guys. We have to
keep playing.

PAUL: Elsa, would you mind singing solo on this one?

GABE: Why?

PAUL: Because I'd like to dance with you.

ELSA: I'd be happy to.

*(*GABE *looks at her. To* GABE*)*

ELSA: Well, go on.

*(*PAUL *draws* GABE *to down center. The mood should be
serene and very Fred and Ginger on the Casino verandah*

in Follow the Fleet *just before they sing and dance*
Let's Face the Music and Dance. *As a matter of fact,*
that's exactly what happens.)

PAUL: I'm sorry.

GABE: I know you are.

(They kiss. PAUL *hums a few bars of* Cheek to Cheek.
GABE *smiles.)*

PAUL: *(Prompting)* Corey.

(COREY *strikes up a sultry tango.* GABE *tries to pull away*
from PAUL, PAUL *draws him back and soon* GABE *succumbs*
to PAUL*'s entreaties and they begin a passionate dance à la*
Let's Face the Music and Dance. *The music is a tango*
dance version of "Misery." ELSA *sings the lyrics. A third of*
the way through the song she is joined by KEGAN, *also in*
formal wear, who dances with her. Eventually CHRISTIAN
and DARRYL *enter, also in formal wear, and the number*
builds to a huge ACT ONE finale with the two central
couples singing and dancing center, COREY *still playing*
the piano and DARRYL *and* CHRISTIAN *serving as elegant*
bookends stage right and stage left to the whole production
number.)

(Blackout)

END OF ACT ONE

ACT TWO

2:1

(The panel shows a palm tree. The act begins with more throbbing disco music. PAUL *and* GABE *and* KEGAN *and* ELSA *are dancing amidst a large group of gyrating men. When the dance ends they move down stage to the steps and sit in a row.* PAUL *has his arms around* GABE *and* KEGAN *has her arms around* ELSA.)

ELSA: That's it. No more dancing in gay clubs. I can't stand all the attitude I get from fags.

KEGAN: That's because you dress like you're straight.

ELSA: If acceptance means dressing like a dyke, forget it. I'll do without dancing.

PAUL: *(Rhetorically)* Isn't Gabriel the cutest thing?

KEGAN: Would you stop saying that over and over again?

PAUL: I can't help it.

GABE: Aren't the palm trees beautiful?

PAUL: Yes, I think they're beautiful.

KEGAN: Isn't Elsa the cutest thing?

ELSA: Stop.

KEGAN: We were wondering if you two wanted to drive down to Big Sur with us this weekend.

PAUL: *(Grandly)* We are at home this weekend.

GABE: *(Also grandly)* And not receiving.

ELSA: You two are amazing. You never go out. This is the first time we've seen you out since the Black and White Ball.

PAUL: There's no need to travel abroad when all you need is at home.

GABE: Paul does best when he's spared the decorum of society.

PAUL: My politics are too demanding. My manner too honest.

KEGAN: *(To* ELSA*)* So what do you think? They're still happy.

ELSA: Oh stop.

GABE: What?

KEGAN: Elsa gave you guys two weeks. Tops. It was her big excuse for not moving in with me. *(To* ELSA*)* They've been together for one year now.

ELSA: Cohabitation ruins relationships.

KEGAN: That is a completely unsophisticated remark which is not borne out by the evidence at hand.

ELSA: Paul has subsumed his personality into Gabriel's. *(To* PAUL*)* I'm right, aren't I?

PAUL: Yes, I've succumbed to the force majeure.

ELSA: Every relationship has a dominant and a passive personality.

PAUL: A top and a bottom.

ELSA: Which means someone always has to lose in a domestic arrangement.

PAUL: Unless you enjoy being the bottom.

(GABE *nudges him.*)

PAUL: I do.

KEGAN: But Paul's personality was abrasive and offensive. It needed subsuming.

PAUL: Here, here.

ELSA: Yes, well, when I have a personality in need of subsuming I will submit to cohabitation.

KEGAN: But I'm willing to submit to you.

ELSA: I don't want that responsibility.

GABE: A wise decision. It's like having a huge baby around.

(*He nudges* PAUL.)

PAUL: (*Hugging* GABE) And a daddy who's always willing to screw the baby.

(*This comment embarrasses* GABE. *He gives* PAUL *a "you never know when to stop" look.*)

KEGAN: Elsa's mother's coming next week. She's going to introduce me as her "friend".

ELSA: Could we not discuss that right now?

PAUL: I'm still "Paul the Roommate" to Gabriel's mother.

KEGAN: That's disgusting. A year ago you would have made it a pre-requisite to intercourse that he tell the whole world he's gay.

PAUL: I've come to accept Gabriel's closet as a necessary transitional tool from late adolescent androgyny to full blown homosexuality. He'll tell his mother eventually. As will Elsa. So long as there's room in his closet for two, I'm happy.

KEGAN: *(To* ELSA*)* So I'll move in and you can introduce me as your roommate.

ELSA: My mother's not that stupid.

GABE: That's right. Mine is kind of stupid.

PAUL: No she's not. She knows, she just appreciates us not shoving it in her face. She gave me a Johnny Mathis album for Christmas. That was her code for "I know. And I've always suspected that Johnny Mathis was too."

GABE: If she meant that, I'm sure she's not aware she meant it. You know what I mean?

PAUL: Like a part of her brain knows that you and I and Johnny Mathis are gay and that was the part that gave me the gift. But another part, the important part, the cerebellum, is in complete denial and doesn't know why the hell she chose Johnny Mathis.

GABE: Yes, she's sending us signals she's not even aware she's sending.

PAUL: Fascinating. Do you think we send signals back?

GABE: Well, let's see. We cooked dinner for her... But that's not a very strong signal that we're gay.

PAUL: Oh, wait. Macy's. We took her to Macy's.

GABE: Oh, yes, on a Sunday morning no less.

PAUL: Oh my God. That's a very strong signal.

GABE: We might as well have kissed in front of her.

PAUL: *(To* KEGAN *and* ELSA*)* So you see, we're out to a part of Gabriel's mother.

GABE: But the other part would shut down the whole apparatus if it was ever directly confronted.

PAUL: We've established a beachhead. Like John Wayne in *The Sands of Iwo Jima.* We must now move inland.

GABE: The perfect metaphor for the outing process.

PAUL: John Wayne speaks to the ages.

2:2

(The lights dim out on PAUL *and* GABE *leaving* ELSA *and* KEGAN *in a spot light on the stairs.)*

KEGAN: *(To the audience)* And so, as we enter the second act, the lesbians are still not living together.

ELSA: *(To the audience)* It's a very small thing.

KEGAN: *(To* ELSA*)* It's not a small thing. It's embarrassing. So far the narrative seems to suggest that only gay men can get their shit together.

ELSA: Yeah, well, I'm not here to advance the lesbian narrative. I told you I was closeted politically. Living together is a political act.

KEGAN: So is sex.

ELSA: Sex is recreational.

KEGAN: If you reduce it to the act of sex and the orgasm, yes, it's recreational. But it is also an expression of sexuality. And any expression of sexuality is a political act.

ELSA: That's silly. Look—I'm not interested in the political component of sex. I'm just interested in the sex. O K?

KEGAN: That is completely archaic. That's like caveman sexuality.

ELSA: No, it's pre-politicized sex.

KEGAN: Pre-politicized sex?

ELSA: Politics has ruined sex. *The Politics of Desire.* It's just stupid. Desire is desire. It's apolitical nature is exactly what makes it unique and important. Add to desire living together and trumpeting to the whole world that you're gay and, I promise you, you've ruined desire.

KEGAN: And graduated to a higher level.

ELSA: Not of desire. Desire is pure and simple.

KEGAN: You like the closet. It makes it more exciting for you.

ELSA: Yes. Excitement is an important component of desire.

KEGAN: You're a sophist

ELSA: No, I just don't feel I have to legitimize my desire by living with you.

KEGAN: Fine, don't legitimize it. *(She turns away.)*

ELSA: *(Making an effort)* But, I was thinking, maybe it's time I told my mother.

KEGAN: That would be great. Your first political act.

ELSA: No, I think I just want to piss her off.

KEGAN: That's a valid motivation. Now living with me...that would really piss her off.

ELSA: We'll see.

2:3

(The spot shifts to COREY *who stands stage right and holds a phone. He is dressed in a white dinner jacket and black tie. He presses the last button and we hear* CHRISTIAN's *voice on an answering machine.)*

CHRISTIAN: *(On the answering machine)* Hi, this is Christian. Leave me a message.

COREY: Hi Chris, this is Corey. Are you there? *(Pause)* Guess not. Just called to say hello and I'll talk to you real soon. Bye.

PAUL: *(Entering from right, also in a dinner jacket and tie)* Corey had made the mistake of falling in love with Christian. Christian responded by screening his calls. *(To* COREY*)* You look great. Now you forget that little prick. Every rich eligible bachelor in town will be here tonight. Look sharp.

*(*GABE *and* DARRYL *enter from left in dinner jackets and ties and cross to center. As they enter, Elsa enters stage right and begins quietly singing* Misery.*)*

GABE: *(To the audience)* Elsa had landed us a gig at the opening of the new Museum of Modern Art.

(The panel in the frame quickly shifts to reveal a Clifford Still painting. GABE *and* DARRYL *eye it critically. To audience)*

GABE: But then she got sick.

*(*ELSA *coughs wildly and exits stage right.)*

GABE: So Elsa sent Darryl.

DARRYL: Who, as it turns out, could sing.

GABE: It was a little strange because Elsa and I used to sing all the love duets.

PAUL: However absurd that might have looked.

DARRYL: So Paul cooked up some new lyrics for us.

COREY: Lyrics of questionable taste.

PAUL: I was currently fascinated by transgenderism.

COREY: Christ was a cross-dresser?

PAUL: "These spikes are killing me."

COREY: But Gabe and Darryl, as it turned out, had chemistry.

GABE: 2:4

(GABE *and* DARRYL *sing* Queer Theory, *which is set to an up-tempo version of* Misery's *melody.*)

GABE:
When your ex
With big pecs
Changes sex
It's queer theory.

DARRYL:
When his chest,
Swells with breasts
You're obsessed
With queer theory!

GABE: Now you're sneaking a peak at things few would

DARRYL: You remember your gender is flu-id

GABE: And the best lover you've got

DARRYL: Is in some ways lacking a lot

GABE/DARRYL: Queer theory, queer theory!

DARRYL: (*Spoken*) Ladies and gentlemen, let's hear if for S F MOMA! (*Cheering*)

When your chick
Who was slick
Gets a dick
It's queer theory.

GABE:
When your man
Who's a Stan
Is now a Fran
Queer theory.

DARRYL:
So you need to read those who know
Try some Butler, Friedan and Foucault

But it's all just dusty old text
In the end you're alone and intersexed.
Queer theory, queer theory.

GABE:
Please don't tell me what you think sex is,
Or how you wish that I could be more normal
I'll ignore the social moral nexus
What I feel is far beyond hormonal.

DARRYL: When your curves

GABE: And your nerves

DARRYL: Start to swerve

GABE/DARRYL: It's queer theory!

GABE: And new hair

DARRYL: Grows everywhere

GABE: Even there!

GABE/DARRYL: Queer theory!

DARRYL: You peruse when you choose where to pee

GABE: Is the men's room the right room for me?

DARRYL: So you just bust through the door,

GABE: A transcender of gender once more

GABE/DARRYL: Queer theory! Queer theory!
Queer theory! Queer theory!

*(They end in an embrace and a kiss on the lips. Applause.
They bow. PAUL, who has been watching, claps
enthusiastically.)*

PAUL: *(Kissing GABE on the cheek)* Gabriel, you were
wonderful as always.

GABE: Thank you Paul

PAUL: *(To* DARRYL*)* And you were just priceless.
Elsa would tear your eyes out if she saw you in
action with her partner.

DARRYL: Thanks Paul.

*(*CHRISTIAN *enters from left in a dinner jacket and black tie.
He holds two champagne glasses and is obviously tipsy.)*

CHRISTIAN: Hi.

(All look at CHRISTIAN. *Silence)*

PAUL: Christian. What a surprise. How are you?
You look terrible. Treating someone badly?
Guilty conscience?

CHRISTIAN: Hi Corey.

COREY: Hi Chris.

PAUL: How sweet. Christian, you remember Darryl.

CHRISTIAN: Hey, man. Nice voice.

DARRYL: Thanks.

PAUL: *(To* CHRISTIAN*)* Darryl is here with Corey.

*(*PAUL *shoves* DARRYL *such that* DARRYL *falls on top of*
COREY*)*

PAUL: They're dating. They've been dating for years.
You were just a fling. Corey was using you for sex.
But Darryl understands and he's forgiven Corey.
(To DARRYL*)* Haven't you Darryl?

DARRYL: *(Reluctantly playing along)* Sure.

CHRISTIAN: Cool.

*(*JANE *enters from left, crosses down stage, then makes some
snorting noises. She is dressed in a slinky cocktail dress,
is nineteen years old, obviously very rich, very spoiled and
very high. She holds a champagne glass.)*

JANE: *(Spotting* CHRISTIAN*)* Christian! There you are. *(She crosses to him and kisses his mouth.)*

CHRISTIAN: *(To the others)* This is Jane.

PAUL: Janey?

JANE: No, just Jane. You must Paul the Drag Queen.

PAUL: No, just Paul. You're here with Christian?

JANE: No, he's here with me. *(Taking the stage)* My uncle practically owns this place. The museum board ran out of money half-way through construction and my uncle's like this sleazy loan-shark type and he put up the rest of the money because he's trying to clean up his name in this town because the police busted him a few months ago sucking off a male hustler in the toilet of the Union Square Garage. And Herb Caen wrote this whole column about it. My uncle told me to bring Christian along because he's in lust with him. He lusts after all my boyfriends. *(To* GABE*)* You have got a great voice, man. *(To* DARRYL*)* Yours is alright. *(To the world)* I love old shit: Cole Porter, Gershwin—George and Ira. My mother listens to it. She lives in West Hollywood. My father lives in Bel Aire. But he's a total asshole. He actually went through this whole youth thing shit and became a fag when he was like forty years old. Now he cruises bars and picks up teenagers and listens to Aretha Franklin and does coke and he is totally old looking and pathetic. He used to work for Paramount until he blew this whole deal with Kate Moss to make her first movie because she decided he was too much of a creepy fag and she couldn't handle it so she told him to fuck off! Kate hates fags. Except Calvin Klein of course. But she's totally fat anyway. They've been keeping it a big secret and now they're sending her to a farm. She's a fucking cow. Moo. *(And she assumes a Kate Moss pose which she holds. Then she acts as if she is being attacked by bats. Slowly she recovers.)*

PAUL: *(After a long pause)* Are you a student at Berkeley?

JANE: No, I go to Stanford.

(They all nod in recognition—of course she goes to Stanford.)

CHRISTIAN: We should split.

PAUL: Oh no, stay. This is fascinating. What a charming young lady you've thrown Corey over for. Now tell me, are you bi-sexual or just straight?

GABE: Paul.

PAUL: *(To GABE)* No, now, I'm interested. *(To CHRISTIAN)* Straight or bi which is it?

JANE: Are you one of those creepy fags who thinks all cute guys like Christian are gay?

PAUL: No, I'm one of those creepy fags who think all cute fags like Christian are gay.

COREY: Paul, please don't do this on my account.

PAUL: Oh, I'm not doing this on your account. I'm doing this for all the self-respecting homosexuals of the world.

COREY: Of course.

JANE: *(Noticing COREY)* Who's that queen at the piano?

PAUL: That's Doctor Cabinoff of the University of California.

JANE: *(To the audience)* Mmm... I like MDs.

PAUL: Actually, he's a PhD.

JANE: *(To the audience)* Mmmm.. I love PhDs.

COREY: Actually, I have both.

JANE: *(Pressing herself against him)* Do you want to dance? Christian can't dance and this conversation's getting really boring.

COREY: *(Uncomfortable)* Actually, you remind me of my first girl friend. When I was straight.

JANE: I love people who were straight. *(She starts to exit.)* If you decide you need a realignment, I'll be at the caviar.

(She sends a nasty bite in COREY's *direction and exits.* COREY *notices something off-stage.)*

COREY: We better start playing again. That guy who hired us is giving us dirty looks.

DARRYL: He's been doing that all night.

ADAM: *(Entering from right)* Ah, hi, we gotta talk.

COREY: We were just taking a little break.

PAUL: They've been receiving plaudits from coke heads.

ADAM: Oh no, that's fine. You see the problem is... *(To* DARRYL*)* Well, weren't you a girl?

GABE: That was Elsa. She couldn't make it.

ADAM: Oh, O K, I thought so. Yeah.

DARRYL: So we're doing it without her.

ADAM: Got it. O K. Yeah. But, ah, one thing. Could you guys maybe back off a little bit. Like, ah, maybe one of you sing at a time or something.

GABE: Why?

ADAM: Well, the two of you singing at once...and those lyrics...it's a little much for this crowd. You know what I mean?

GABE: You're kidding me?

ADAM: Hey, look, I just book the acts. O K? I think you guys sound great. My boyfriend over there thinks you sound great. But most of the people here tonight are pretty uptight. You know, straight, middle-aged,

conservative art patrons. And the Boy-Boy Love Act's
a bit too intense for this crowd.

GABE: *(Annoyed but complacent)* O K. Fine. Whatever.
We'll only sing solos. No duets.

PAUL: Oh please. Half the people here tonight are fags.

ADAM: Well, maybe, but it still isn't right for this crowd.

PAUL: Oh for Christ's sake. This is San Francisco.
Of course it's *right* for this crowd. It would be obscene
if it was anything but a boy loves boy routine.

GABE: Paul.

PAUL: I've only seen two kinds of men here tonight—
fags with wives and *(With a look towards* CHRISTIAN*)*
fags without wives. And then, of course, there are the
artists, organizers, journalists and local celebs, queens
every one of them.

ADAM: And who the hell are you?

PAUL: I'm a concerned homosexual who does not
believe that you, a fag, should be telling them, also fags,
that they can't perform for a predominantly fag
audience.

ADAM: This is not a predominantly fag audience.

PAUL: All right, Mary, a predominantly closeted
audience.

ADAM: Fine, a closeted audience. I don't give a shit.
(To GABE*)* Just sing solos. O K? No duets. And nothing
faggy. O K? *(And he exits.)*

PAUL: Absolutely unbelievable.

GABE: Just forget it Paul.

PAUL: I will not forget it. It's outrageous. This is the
Museum of Modern Art. If fags haven't made a

contribution to modern art I don't know who has. Your act is a tribute to the works that grace these halls.

GABE: Would you please relax?

PAUL: *(Grabbing the mike from* DARRYL*)* I will not relax. Give me that mike. *(To* COREY*)* Do you know *Love for Sale*?

COREY: Yes, but I'm not playing it.

PAUL: Fine, then I'll sing it a cappella. *(Into the microphone as if he were speaking to the museum at large)* Ladies and gentlemen, I'd like to welcome you to the new and beautiful Museum of Modern Art. This next number is dedicated to those great *homosexual* modern artists like Jasper Johns and Robert Rauschenberg. This song was written by that great *homosexual* composer Cole Porter. It's one of my very favorites and I hope you like it too.
(He performs Love for Sale *with explicit gestures.)*
Love for sale.
Appetizing young male love for sale.
Love that's fresh and still unspoiled.
Love that's only slightly soiled.
Love—

(And the stage lights and the microphone power are turned off.)

PAUL: *(In the dark)* Oh hell.

(The lights come back up slowly.)

GABE: Well, so much for that.

COREY: Fucking unbelievable.

PAUL: A blow for freedom!

DARRYL: You've got a nice voice.

PAUL: A star is born.

(CHRISTIAN *falls drunkenly onto the floor with a tremendous crash.*)

DARRYL: Jesus.

GABE: Is he all right?

COREY: He's drunk. Passed out. I think he's fine.

PAUL: A triumphant evening all around.

COREY: *(Lifting* CHRISTIAN's *head)* Chris?

CHRISTIAN: Casey?

COREY: Corey. *(To* PAUL*)* I think we better get him home.

PAUL: Isn't that Janey's responsibility?

DARRYL: She's seems to be humping a Rauschenberg.

(*We hear* JANE *groaning off-stage.*)

COREY: Let's go. This gig's a dog.

PAUL: Again I'm the villain. *(To* GABE*)* Are you coming?

GABE: *(Pissed)* No. I'll get home on BART. I'll see you later.

COREY: Paul. Can we go? I want to leave before he starts vomiting.

(COREY *and* PAUL, *supporting* CHRISTIAN, *exit stage right. Just after they leave the stage we hear* CHRISTIAN *vomit.*)

PAUL: *(Off-stage)* Oh my God.

2:5

(*Immediately we hear a recording of Johnny Mathis singing* Misty.)

DARRYL: We've been replaced. *(He listens.)* Johnny Mathis.

(DARRYL *and* GABE *stare at one another while the music plays. It is a moment held a little too long.*)

GABE: *(Suddenly feeling uncomfortable)* We should go. *(To the audience)* So we walked to BART in silence.

(The spot light races across the wall of the theatre and arrives down center on the steps. It is accompanied by a train whistle. DARRYL *surreptitiously makes the sound of the BART doors opening and closing. They sit on the steps and the stage lights blackout leaving them in the spot light. We hear a very garbled announcement over the BART P A. They nod their heads as if they understood.*)

GABE: And somewhere between 12th and 19th Streets Oakland I felt I should apologize to Darryl. *(To* DARRYL*)* I'm sorry about that.

DARRYL: About what?

GABE: About Paul. He tends to get drunk and then he goes after anybody he thinks is a closet case—

DARRYL: Hey, don't- I mean, you don't have to apologize for him.

GABE: *(Defensively)* I'm not—I'm— Actually, I'm just saying I'm sorry it happened. *(To the audience)* Actually, I was trying to dissociate myself from Paul. He had again embarrassed me in front of everybody and when I realized what I was doing, I felt like shit.

(Awkward pause)

DARRYL: *(To* GABE*)* I had a great time tonight. I never get to sing to such a large audience.

GABE: You're kidding. You do it so well.

DARRYL: Well, I had a good partner.

(They laugh.)

DARRYL: So, are you coming to see me dance?

GABE: You dance?

DARRYL: Yeah, I'm going to be in the show with Elsa that's coming up. She'd never say anything about it. She's very shy about her dancing.

GABE: Why?

DARRYL: She sucks. *(Pause)* No. I'm kidding. She's just nervous about what we have to do in this dance. You see, she plays an Indian squaw and I'm this Indian brave and it's very sexual.

GABE: It sounds totally stupid.

DARRYL: It is. But this choreographer is in love with Elsa and he likes to see us go at it every night in rehearsal. I'm his stand-in. It's very steamy.

GABE: Does Kegan know about all this?

DARRYL: Oh yes, she's playing the tom-tom for us. She comes to rehearsals all the time. I think the choreographer thinks she's my girlfriend.

GABE: Do you have a girlfriend? *(To the audience)* I don't know why I asked that question.

DARRYL: *(To GABE)* No. I get off here.

GABE: *(Misunderstanding him)* Excuse me?

DARRYL: The train. This is my stop.

GABE: *(Embarrassed at his mistake)* Oh, yes.

DARRYL: I want you and Paul to come and see the show. I'll send you a flier. Now promise you'll come.

GABE: I promise.

DARRYL: And thanks again for a wonderful evening. I had a great time tonight and you were a wonderful partner.

2:6

(He rakishly throws his dinner jacket over his shoulder and exits singing "Misty." As he goes he, of course, makes the sounds of the door opening and closing for him.)

GABE: *(To the audience)* He didn't say a word about Paul's behavior on either occasion. A perfect gentleman.

(We hear a Pet Shop Boys song and PAUL *comes on dancing about the stage. The stage lights come up with his entrance. The picture shifts to an all black panel.)*

GABE: The next morning Paul was up bright and early and dancing about to Pet as if nothing had happened. I was going to give him some sort of a lecture, but how could I when he looked so cute.

PAUL: *(To the audience)* I was subsequently coerced into attending a university dance concert.

KEGAN: *(Entering from left)* You were not coerced. You came willingly. You said you wanted to see Elsa dance.

PAUL: I lied. I wanted to see Darryl, that little fag, in tights.

GABE: *(Offended)* He's not a fag.

*(*KEGAN *and* PAUL *look at each other and say "ooooo". They obviously touched a nerve. Then* PAUL, KEGAN *and* GABE *walk off the stage and take three seats in the theater's auditorium.)*

PAUL: *(To the audience)* It was presented in this cramped stuffy theater with no air-conditioning. *(Or some such reference to whatever theater in which the play is actually being performed.)*

GABE: Which piece is she in?

KEGAN: *The Passion of Little Feather.* I'm on drums.

PAUL: *(Mocking)* *The Passion of Little Feather.* I assume it's all about the love of Elsa, a blushing squaw, for Darryl, a virile brave.

KEGAN: Something like that. Elsa looks great in her costume.

PAUL: How's her dancing?

KEGAN: *(Making a negative noise)* Neh.

GABE: *(Looking around the theatre)* It's a cute theatre.

KEGAN: They did *Tamburlaine* in here last semester.

PAUL: How was it?

KEGAN: Very campy. You would have loved it.

COREY: *(Entering from right)* Hi guys.

PAUL: Corey!

COREY: *(Surprised)* Oh, hi Paul.

PAUL: All is forgiven I trust.

COREY: *(Nervously)* Ah, yes.

(He is joined by ADAM *who is now dressed casually.* ADAM *puts his arms around* COREY's *waist.)*

COREY: This is Adam, who you probably remember from the other night.

PAUL: *(Disgusted)* I don't believe it.

GABE: *(Extending his hand)* Hi.

ADAM: Hi. No hard feelings huh?

PAUL: *(To* COREY*)* Where the hell did you find him? Under a rock?

COREY: I met him last night at The Stud.

PAUL: You don't got to The Stud.

COREY: Well I did last night.

PAUL: *(To* ADAM*)* I thought you had a boyfriend.

GABE: Paul.

COREY: Would you relax?

PAUL: If anyone else tells me to relax I swear to God I'm going to strangle him.

KEGAN: What's gong on?

PAUL: *(Referring to* ADAM*)* This is the queen from the museum opening who shut down their act because he thought it was too queeny.

COREY: No, he shut down your act. Our act was fine.

PAUL: And now Corey, having a surprisingly short memory and very little tact, has decided to parade him around campus.

COREY: I should have known this was a mistake.

PAUL: Yes, you should have. I can't believe you brought him here.

COREY: I meant I should have known it was a mistake to bring him down here and try and introduce him to you. I'm playing in this concert and he's my guest.

PAUL: Then why did you introduce him?

COREY: *(Sarcastic)* Well I thought you might be civil about this. I forgot you were a member of the homosexual Gestapo. *(To* ADAM*)* I'm sorry about this.

ADAM: That's O K.

(They kiss.)

PAUL: I might vomit. This is completely amazing to me. How can you be dating this person?

ADAM: *(To* PAUL. *Smarmy)* Look. What happened the other night—that was business. I happen to think the act was very good and, believe it or not, I respect your passion. I really do. If it had been a different venue, an opening in the Castro or even in SOMA. I would have had no problem with any of it. Hey, I'm gay.

PAUL: *(To the audience, pointing to* ADAM*)* This person is unacceptable. *(To the others)* If he doesn't leave right now I'm going to scream the house down. *(To* ADAM*)* I want you out of my site.

ADAM: What the hell is this, a John Wayne movie?

PAUL: Yeah, it's a John Wayne movie. Get the fuck out of town.

COREY: *(Furious)* You are psychotic. This is not your town. It belongs to the people of California.

PAUL: A faggot state of which I am a representative.

COREY: *(Pointing to* ADAM*)* So is he.

PAUL: He's not a faggot. He's a heterosexual infiltrator in the faggot community. He's a double agent. A spy. A mole.

CHRISTIAN: *(Entering from right)* Corey.

COREY: Chris?

CHRISTIAN: *(Holding out a flower)* Hi.

PAUL: *(Waving his arms about in manufactured indignation)* Oh great. Another one of Corey's heterosexual lovers. Now the picture is complete.

GABE: Paul!

PAUL: What?

GABE: Could you please go home. *(Pause)* I came to see this show and I'd like it if you just went home now.

PAUL: You're going to let—

GABE: Please!

(PAUL, *recognizing that* GABE *is serious, exits in a huff and mumbling to himself.*)

COREY: He's incredible.

GABE: *(Taking charge)* You get to your piano.

(COREY *goes to the piano.*)

KEGAN: Good work Gabriel.

GABE: You get to your drums.

(KEGAN *goes to her drums.*)

ADAM: Hey, I'm sor—

GABE: You sit down.

(GABE *throws* ADAM *into one of the chairs.* GABE *then realizes that* CHRISTIAN *is trying to talk to* COREY *at the piano.*)

GABE: *(Impatiently)* Christian. *(He grabs* CHRISTIAN *by the hair and throws him into one of the seats.* COREY *and* KEGAN *begin playing the* Passion of Little Feather *vamp. It sounds like "Indian" music.*)

2:7

COREY: *(To the audience)* The People's Ecumenical Dance Theatre presents...

KEGAN: *(To the audience)* "The Passion of Little Feather." A Native-American Tragedy. By Leo Freidman.

(COREY *and* KEGAN *play the music for "The Passion of Little Feather," an absurd little modern dance presentation, which is danced with undergraduate solemnity by* ELSA *and* DARRYL. *Though ridiculous, it is in fact a very steamy little dance. Throughout the dance* GABE *speaks to the audience. In these moments he appears in a spotlight. Although the*

*music stops for his speeches, the dance continues, and the
music resumes whenever he stops speaking.)*

GABE: *(To the audience)* Berkeley, 1995. I was gay.
I wasn't single. I was watching someone dance.

(The music resumes.)

GABE: When do you fall in love? Impossible to say.
And I can't say that I was in love that first time I saw
him dance. But I was transfixed.

*(The music resumes. Then the dance ends and the stage goes
black. GABE jumps to his feet and cheers wildly. The stage
lights come up and DARRYL and ELSA come out to take their
bows. DARRYL looks at GABE during the bows and smiles.
At this moment GABE speaks to the audience and everybody
freezes.)*

GABE: When do you fall in love with somebody?
(He points to the frozen DARRYL.) That's when you fall in
love with somebody. There's the moment. Right there.
Adorable. Completely adorable.

*(The curtain call ends and DARRYL and ELSA run off stage
right.)*

2:8

GABE: *(To the audience)* So I rushed back-stage to wax
poetic on Darryl's performance.

*(The stage lights come up and GABE crosses to up center.
ELSA and KEGAN cross the stage from right to left without
seeing GABE.)*

ELSA: *(To KEGAN)* So, what did you think?

KEGAN: You were great. Darryl sucked.

(And they are off.)

(Meanwhile ADAM *and* CHRISTIAN *have joined* COREY *at the piano.)*

COREY: So, what did you think?

ADAM: You were great. The dancers sucked.

CHRISTIAN: *(Pitifully)* I liked the dancers.

*(*ADAM *gives* CHRISTIAN *a nasty look and* CHRISTIAN *exits right.* ADAM *puts his arms around* COREY. COREY *plays a slow love song under the next stretch of dialogue.* DARRYL *enters from right wearing a terry-cloth bathrobe and holding a single red rose. He meets* GABE *up center.)*

DARRYL: *(To* GABE*)* Hey, man.

GABE: *(To the audience)* Darryl, that was great. Just great. It was just great. Great. It was so...great.

(There is a pause.)

DARRYL: So you liked it?

GABE: Yes, I thought it was great. No, I thought it was wonderful. Better than wonderful. Great. *(To the audience)* He knew I was in love with him.

DARRYL: *(To audience, sarcastic)* I had no idea.

GABE: *(To* DARRYL*)* Who gave you the flower?

DARRYL: This? Elsa.

GABE: I wish I had something to give you. I didn't expect you to be any good. No, I mean...you know. I thought you'd be fine. I mean, I thought you'd be good. I thought you'd be nice...I thought you'd be nice. But you were...you were... *(He trails off and just stares.)*

DARRYL: Great?

GABE: *(Snapping out of it)* Yes, you were great. And I wish I had something to give you.

DARRYL: How about a kiss?

(The music abruptly stops. Silence.)

GABE: *(Stunned)* What?

DARRYL: How about a kiss?

GABE: *(To audience)* What? *(To* DARRYL *with utmost sincerity)* I'd love to give you a kiss.

DARRYL: *(Suddenly nervous)* Like a congratulatory kiss.

GABE: Yeah, I understand. I wasn't going to stick my tongue down your throat.

(They move their lips towards each other. At the last moment GABE *turns and addresses the audience. He never actually makes contact.)*

GABE: It was a little kiss. A peck. Not worth recreating. But for me—the world stopped spinning. I actually closed my eyes in the middle of it. Which was a little embarrassing because he pulled away before I could reopen them. Then he must have figured it out.

*(*GABE *resumes his position with his lips extended towards* DARRYL's. DARRYL *pulls back and looks at* GABE *frozen in this absurd position.)*

DARRYL: *(To audience)* Uh, yeah.

GABE: *(To* DARRYL*)* Well, you really were very special tonight. I'm so... Well, I'm not your father so I can't be proud of you but I was just very moved, very impressed, very...proud. So goodnight. I have to go home. *(He begins to back away.)*

DARRYL: *(Handing* GABE *the rose)* Here.

GABE: *(Overwhelmed)* Thank you.

DARRYL: Did Paul like the show?

GABE: *(No idea who he's talking about)* Paul?

DARRYL: Paul.

GABE: Oh, Paul. Yes, yes. He loved it. He had to leave before it started, but he thought it was great. Well, I should go so... Bye.

DARRYL: 'Night.

(DARRYL crosses up to up center. PAUL enters from right and crosses to down right.)

2:9

PAUL: *(To audience)* And so the narrative shifts to Gabriel. In a moment, what was our story becomes his story.

(GABE enters from left and crosses to down left.)

GABE: *(To PAUL)* It didn't happen that quickly.

PAUL: *(To GABE)* Of course it did. It didn't manifest itself that quickly, but that's the night I lost you. I never would have left the theatre if I'd known this would have happened.

GABE: It would have happened anyway.

PAUL: But maybe not as soon.

DARRYL: *(To the audience as he crosses down center)* Gabe told me everything. About how much he loved Paul and how guilty he felt even talking to me. He felt even this was a betrayal.

GABE: *(As he crosses to meet DARRYL down center)* And he told me how I shouldn't worry about it because he wasn't actually gay.

DARRYL: He never hit on me or made me feel closeted because I wouldn't touch him.

GABE: And I never really cared whether or not he was gay. Maybe he wasn't. He just made me feel good.

DARRYL: Just as he made me feel good.

GABE: And then one night.

DARRYL: I can't even tell you who initiated it.

(DARRYL *and* GABE *kiss as* PAUL *looks on.*)

PAUL: *(To the audience)* When I was nineteen years old I fell in love with a man seven years older than me. He'd been actively gay since he was fifteen and he spotted me as a virgin even before I spoke to him. We slept together and only afterwards did my anxiety about being homosexual set in. He told me it was a stupid thing to worry about because in America in the 1980s nobody intelligent had any hang-ups about sexual orientation. To be gay was the hippest, the most stylish, the most progressive thing a person could be. He told me straight was conventional, gay was progressive. And when I slept with someone else for the first time I told him that monogamy was also conventional, sleeping around was progressive. I told him that he had created me. He'd made it all right to be gay. And I told him that he had to allow his creation to go on exploring the nature of his own sexuality. And monogamy was not one of its manifestations. Four years later I sat on my living room floor and listened to Gabriel say the same things to me.

(DARRYL *exits and* PAUL *and* GABE *sit on the stairs down center.*)

GABE: *(To* PAUL*)* I'm only sorry it took so long for me to tell you.

PAUL: You didn't tell me. I found out.

GABE: I can't believe you were spying on me.

PAUL: Of course I was spying on you. That's how I met you in the first place. Kegan and I were spying on Elsa.

GABE: No. We met at Flore. You laughed at me when
I said I was straight.

PAUL: And guess what? I was right. You weren't
straight.

GABE: Only because you made me feel like it was ok to
be gay.

PAUL: No. I made you feel it was ok to be my boyfriend.
It wasn't an altruistic act. I am not your therapist and
I am certainly not your daddy. I never expected you
to knock off the first cute twink in a unitard to come
mincing across your path.

GABE: Well I guess there's more to my identity than
"Paul's boyfriend".

PAUL: Apparently. There's "Paul's boyfriend" and
there's "Darryl's boyfriend" and Christ knows who else.

GABE: There's nobody else. That's it. How the hell was
I supposed to tell you about this?

PAUL: You're right—much better strategy: never
tell me. Just carry on with the two of us indefinitely.
That seems like a very rational solution to the problem.

GABE: Much better solution. Deny my feelings about
Darryl. That's cheating. Cheating's immoral. Oh, and
while I'm at it, deny my feelings about Paul. That's gay.
Gay is immoral.

PAUL: So debunk all conventional morality? You wanna
kill someone, go ahead and kill 'em. If you get the chair
it's not because something is inherently wrong about it,
it's because society's uptight.

GABE: And that's what I've done? Killed someone.

PAUL: I can't imagine death is much more painful than
what I'm feeling right now.

GABE: *(To audience)* And the clichés flew all weekend. *(To* PAUL*)* I mean the words were cliché, not the feelings.

PAUL: *(To the audience)* Eventually I told him I thought I could live with it. I was hoping his feelings for Darryl would pass.

GABE: *(To the audience)* I knew they wouldn't. But who can pass up the chance to have two lovers. It was incredibly exciting. It also felt incredibly selfish. Like I was torturing him. And, sick as it may sound, that too was very exciting.

PAUL: *(To audience)* Historically, I should have killed him. Killed him and his lover. And then killed myself. Or better yet, slay his son and then myself like Butterfly. Or, this is best, kill both his sons and his lover and fly off in my chariot laughing maniacally like Medea.

GABE: *(To* PAUL*)* But we were never blessed with issue.

PAUL: *(To* GABE*)* You should have drowned before you could betray me like Antnous.

GABE: Or died defending your honor like Patroclus.

PAUL: Or we should have lusted for each other but never slept together like Socrates and Alcibiades.

*(*PAUL *and* GABE *think for a moment.)*

GABE: Nahhhh.

PAUL: I never bought that anyway. How could Socrates have kept his hands off Alcibiades? Alcibiades was supposed to have been a total stud.

GABE: He was probably afraid Alcibiades would betray him.

PAUL: I still don't know how he could resist it. I'm sure it would have been worth the pain of losing him.

*(*PAUL *and* GABE *embrace.)*

PAUL: *(To the audience)* A few days later Gabriel moved out.

(GABE stands and crosses to down right.)

GABE: *(To the audience)* And Paul put me through all the trials of an ugly break-up.

PAUL: It wasn't that bad.

GABE: *(To PAUL)* Oh please. *(To audience)* He'd get drunk and make abusive phone calls.

PAUL: *(Suddenly drunk)* You fucking asshole!

GABE: Then he'd sober up and apologize.

PAUL: *(Suddenly sober)* I'm sorry.

GABE: Then he'd make abusive sober phone calls.

PAUL: How's Darryl? Has he cheated on you yet?

GABE: Then he'd get drunk and apologize.

PAUL: *(Drunk)* I'm sorry.

GABE: Then he'd beg me to tell him what he did wrong.

PAUL: *(To GABE)* I embarrassed you, didn't I?

GABE: *(To PAUL)* It's not that simple. *(To the audience)* But the worst was the constant begging me to come back to him.

PAUL: *(To GABE)* Can I at least take you out? To dinner?

GABE: *(To PAUL)* No. *(To the audience)* He drank too much. He listened to too much Billie Holiday.

(We hear Billie Holiday singing I'm a Fool to Want You. *PAUL weeps uncontrollably. COREY enters from left and crosses to just right of PAUL.)*

2:10

GABE: *(To audience)* And then one day he announced to Corey.

PAUL: I have no intention of finishing the program. My boyfriend has left me and consequently I have no interest in Roman faggots or Greek faggots or Christian faggots or Medieval faggots or history in general. I'm quitting the university. *(Deeply self-lacerating)* I'm going to work in a bookstore. Not a cool one like City Lights. I'm going to get a job at Walden's. Or Barnes and Noble. *(Hitting bottom)* Maybe even Crown. *(He sobs.)*

COREY: *(Trying hard to be nice)* Gabriel left you?

PAUL: *(Through the tears)* Yes.

COREY: I'm sorry.

PAUL: So I guess this is good-bye.

COREY: No. You must complete your dissertation. It is very important work.

PAUL: You're kidding?

COREY: No. Outlandish as your premise might be, if you don't write about it no one else will. Get it published properly and you'll stir things up quite a bit.

PAUL: You're encouraging me to write about a gay Christ?

COREY: Well, why not? We've had every other kind of Christ. It seems to me a gay one is long overdue.

PAUL: *(Breaking down again)* But I'm miserable.

COREY: But that's good for a writer. Misery fuels great writing.

PAUL: *(Incredulous)* What?

COREY: Best book I ever wrote? After my second divorce. I was twenty-two. So young. *(The thought causes him to sniffle.)*

PAUL: Thank you.

COREY: Good luck.

(And she slaps PAUL on the back with such force that PAUL falls forward. COREY exits quickly left trying to hold back the tears. GABE sits on the right edge of the stairs and PAUL stands down center.)

GABE: *(To audience)* So Paul, miserable throughout, wrote a wonderful book. And he became fabulously famous.

2:11

PAUL: *(Speaking as if he were at a huge press conference)* Yes, in the back.

VOICE #1: *(From the back of the auditorium)* How do you feel about your book being banned in both Rome and the state of Utah?

PAUL: Oh, I think it's wonderful. It's great publicity. *(Pointing to someone else)* Yes?

VOICE #2: *(Also from the back)* How do you feel about Tarantino's upcoming movie version of your book?

PAUL: Oh I'm very excited about it. I think Kate Moss will make a terrific Mary Magdalene. And super that Calvin Klein's doing the costumes. Yes.

VOICE #1: Do you see yourself as a gay Jesus? As a prophet of gay permissiveness?

PAUL: Yes, I do as a matter of fact. You're the first to make that connection. Thank you. Yes.

VOICE #2: What are you working on now?

PAUL: *(Coyly)* I'm writing a new book. About Gandhi. *(He licks his lips suggestively.)*

(We hear the Entertainment Tonight Theme as PAUL *crosses to a chaise lounge which has been set up for him down left.* ADAM *is in attendance.* PAUL *sips from an elaborate tropical booze cocktail.)*

PAUL: *(To* ADAM*)* That was exhausting.

ADAM: *(Reading from a daily planner.)* Now let's see... You have your hair treatment at three.

*(*PAUL *examines his hairline.)*

ADAM: Your meeting at Paramount I moved back to 4:30. And we should be at the Grammies by six. Quincy wants you to sing *Love for Sale*.

PAUL: Thank you, Adam.

*(*PAUL *and* ADAM *kiss on the lips. To the audience)*

PAUL: Fame eased the sting of loneliness. As for those I left behind. They were all very happy.

(The cast now sings After the Show *in its entirety. The song begins as a duet between* DARRYL *and* GABE *who sit in each other's arms at the right end of the stairs.* COREY *plays at the piano and sings along with them.* CHRISTIAN *enters and joins the trio as he crosses to the piano and hands* COREY *a flower. Finally* JANE *enters holding a large mirror and singing to her own image. Near the end of the song* KEGAN *and* ELSA *enter from left dribbling a basketball. Just as the song ends they stop dribbling the ball. They end up just left of center.* KEGAN *has her arms around* ELSA's *waist. They look out over the audience.)*

KEGAN: So, what do you think?

ELSA: It's huge. What was it?

KEGAN: A warehouse. They stored pianos here. Now you can set up over there. And I'll set up over here. And it'll be like we live in two separate apartments.

ELSA: And maybe we can move them a little closer together every month.

KEGAN: We'll begin with a trial separation and work towards marriage.

ELSA: It's such a beautiful view of the Bay.

KEGAN: Mmmm. You told your mother about me?

ELSA: Yes.

KEGAN: What did she say?

ELSA: She didn't approve. *(Pause)* You're not Jewish.

(They both laugh.)

KEGAN: Do that thing with your hair.

ELSA: What, this thing? *(And she does it as she speaks.)*

KEGAN: *(Overwhelmed as before)* Uhhh. Adorable.

(They kiss deeply. The basketball falls and rolls away from them, maybe into the audience—that's O K.)

PAUL: *(To audience)* Joy is a state that transcend happiness. I'm happy now on my chaise in the sun. But there was one year when I knew that transcendent joy. And every now and then I look to the north, to that little star on the bay, and I think, without regret, of Gabriel. He was love. He was happiness. He was joy. Corey.

(COREY strikes a chord. The cast sings After the Show *in up-tempo.)*

PAUL: The thing about longing,
It won't let you rest.

GABE/DARRYL: It sticks in your side,
It burns in your chest.

ALL: *(In an up tempo)*
For some love's a fire,
For me it's a scorch,
Aflame with desire,
I carry your torch.

PAUL: *(Spoken)* Ooooo... Hot!

ALL: Even after the show,
You don't have to act.
The fiction you know,
Now let's live the fact.
While others go home,
To fortune and fame

PAUL: *(Back into slow tempo)*
I stand here alone

ALL: *(Slow tempo)*
And whisper your name.

(Blackout)

END OF PLAY